IRELAND

IN OLD PHOTOGRAPHS

T0333256

DONEGAL

SEÁN BEATTIE

The
History
Press

First published in 2004 by
Sutton Publishing Limited

Reprinted 2004

Reprinted in 2008 by
The History Press
The Mill, Brimscombe Port,
Stroud, Gloucestershire, GL5 2QG
www.thehistorypress.co.uk

Reprinted 2010

British Library Cataloguing in Publication Data
A catalogue record for this book is available from the
British Library.

ISBN 978-0-7509-3825-9

Typeset in 10.5/13.5 Photina.
Typesetting and origination by
Sutton Publishing Limited.
Printed and bound in England.

Title page photograph: Market Day in Letterkenny. Cattle are driven through the town past Market Square in the early years of the nineteenth century. The only vehicles to be seen are a cart and an open car. The horse would have been stabled nearby. A market stall can be seen in the Square. This picture is a useful reminder of the rural origins of the town as a centre for local markets, farmers and traders from surrounding areas. (*McClintock Collection*)

An Tostal Parade, 1950s. An Tostal was planned as a national celebration in 1953 in an effor to promote Irish culture and tourism throughout the country. This section of the Tostal Parade i Letterkenny's Main Street is devoted to farm machinery, with tractors, horse-drawn machinery and scythe representing traditional farming methods. The business premises on the right is the Drum Ba *(McClintock Collection)*

CONTENTS

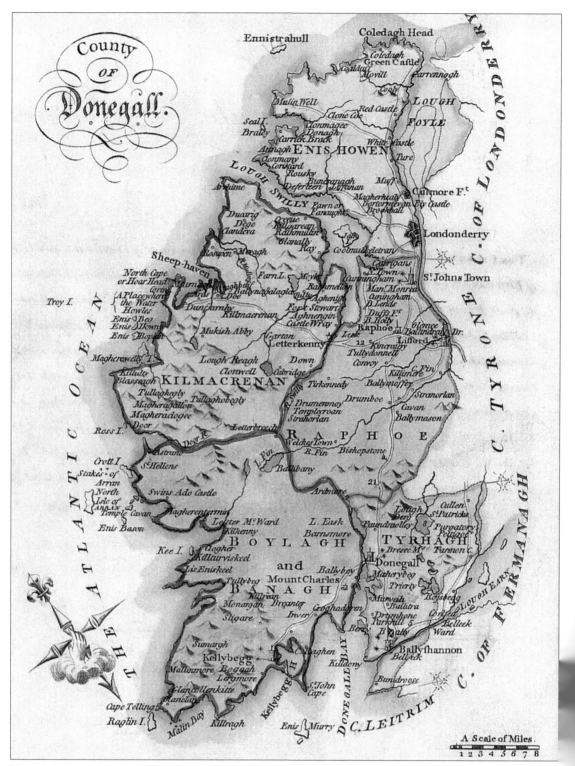

Map of Donegal by Bernard Scale, Land Surveyor, dated 1 February 1776. It is taken from *An Hibernian Atlas or General Description of the Kingdom of Ireland*, which was published by Robert Laurie and J.A. Whittle of 35 Fleet Street, London, in May 1798, as successors to the late Robert Sayer map and print publisher, also of Fleet Street. The map shows the baronies of the county. Following the Local Government Act of 1898, these ceased to exist as administrative units and each county was divided into urban and rural districts. *(Beattie Collection)*

INTRODUCTION

Nineteenth-century directories describe Donegal as a maritime county in the province of Ulster, bounded on the north and west by the Atlantic ocean, on the east by Lough Foyle, Derry and Tyrone, and on the south by Fermanagh and Leitrim. From Inishowen Head in the north to Malinbeg the length of the county is approximately a hundred miles. The original name for the county, excluding Inishowen, was Tír Chonaill, which was derived from Conall, the son of the ruling fifth-century monarch, Niall of the Nine Hostages. His other son, Eoghan, gave his name to the Inishowen peninsula. With the extension of English influence in Elizabethan times the county was 'shired' (designated a county) in 1585 and given the name Dún na nGall, which means the Fort of the Foreigner.

Donegal covers some 1,197,153 acres but less than half of it is suitable for farming. As a coastal county with safe sea inlets and large areas of woodland, it was an attractive place for neolithic farmers and the shell middens or pits and flint factories are evidence of their presence. With the arrival of the Celts and other settlers in the pre-Christian era, a diverse range of stone monuments appeared on the landscape, leaving a rich archaeological heritage of standing stones, stone circles, cist graves and megalithic tombs. The coming of Christianity in the fifth century saw the introduction of monastic settlements. A variety of cross-slabs, high crosses and holy wells representing the new religion replaced the sacred wooded shrines of the Druids. The county also proved an attractive landing-place for Viking warriors, who tried to establish settlements along the coast at inland loughs, but these were overpowered by native chieftains who built castles and ring forts to secure their territories. The introduction of English, Scottish and Welsh settlers in the early seventeenth century brought further changes in the landscape, culture and society of the county, and after the so-called Flight of the Earls from Rathmullan in 1607 the old Gaelic order, long dominated by great families such as the O'Donnells and the McSweeneys, came to an end. New administrative structures gradually came into place with influential local landlord families wielding considerable power.

In the nineteenth century Donegal saw periods of social unrest over tithes, rents and farm leases. Towards the end of the century evictions took place during what became known as the Land War, while the Great Famine saw people dying in their thousands. Those who survived flocked to the workhouses or emigrated from the ports of Derry and Ballyshannon. The pre-Famine period saw the county's population reach a peak of 296,448 but by 1956 it had declined to 122,059.

The rugged and beautiful scenery in the county became more accessible to visitors in the nineteenth century when the roads were improved and railways built.

Gate pillars at Burt, 1955. Corn sheaves are grouped in clusters called 'stooks'. The circular stone pillars and the iron gate are familiar landmarks in the Donegal countryside. (*Derry Journal Newspapers*)

Samuel Carter Hall and his wife were impressed by its 'surpassing beauty' when they undertook their tour of Ireland in the 1840s. In succeeding decades seaside villages such as Bundoran, Moville, Buncrana and Rosapenna grew in importance as bathing places and holiday resorts, although Slieve League, the Poisoned Glen and Tory Island were regarded as inaccessible for all but the most adventurous of travellers. By the end of the nineteenth century there were a number of elegant hotels, such as the Rosapenna Hotel, Kees Hotel in Stranorlar, Lough Swilly Hotel in Buncrana and the Imperial in Ballyshannon.

The age of photography was just beginning and photographers were among the patrons of the hotels, attracted by the magnificence of the scenery. Hotel owners were keen to purchase their pictures and display them in their foyers, to be viewed by their clientele who, by and large, were from wealthy backgrounds. This explains the disproportionate number of images of the Rosapenna Hotel, its golf club and its environs in the Lawrence Collection in the National Library in Dublin. Fortunately for us, Donegal was the most photographed of the nine counties of Ulster.

The first photograph in Ireland is believed to have been taken by Francis Beatty, a Belfast engraver, in 1840. At this time photography was the preserve of chemists, engravers and engineers. Little is known about one of the earliest photographers in the north-west, Robert McGee of Derry, but there were itinerant photographers operating in Donegal in the 1850s. Some evidence of their work may be found in diaries of the period. One unpublished diarist, Jane Harvey of Culdaff, recorded the following: 'September 14th 1854. George Harvey came over to tell us that a daguerre-type likeness was to be taken at Malin Hall, so we all went before dinner.'

They must have been impressed because on 11 September the following year she recorded that 'the whole party set out for Malin to have a likeness taken.' Dinner on this occasion was served early and two phaetons were engaged to bring the entire household from Culdaff to Malin Hall for the great event. The first photograph taken at Culdaff House was in 1863 and can be seen in Amy Young's book, *Three Hundred Years in Inishowen*. The use of dry-plate negatives in the 1880s made photography a commercially viable proposition and Donegal residents were able to visit studios in Derry to have their portraits taken. This collection contains many images that were taken in various photographic studios in the city, in the late 1870s and early 1880s. They have been supplied from the archives of David Bigger, who, along with the late Terry McDonald, rescued many invaluable plate-glass negatives from destruction.

Donegal is fortunate that so many great photographers spent so much time in the county. The Lawrence Collection contains over seven hundred high-quality images of the county from the 1880s onwards. Robert Welsh (1859–1936) was employed by the Congested Districts Board to take photographs illustrating the level of poverty that the board had to deal with. These were taken to London to persuade Parliament to provide finance for the board's work. William Green (1870–1958) was a Newry Quaker with an interest in landscape photography; he also recorded people at work in spinning mills, in the woollen industry and in carpet-making in Killybegs.

Sunday break, *c.* 1947. Three Letterkenny ladies – Chrissie Patterson, Edith McClintock and May McClintock-Wells – enjoy an afternoon stroll in the Laggan countryside. The toddler is Billy Patterson, now a director of Highland Radio, and once a member of one of Donegal's most famous singing groups, the Pattersons. They were a regular feature on RTE, BBC and ITV in the 1960s and 1970s and also had a regular slot on *The Morecambe and Wise Show*. (*McClintock Collection*)

Newspapers were slow to see the value of photography but the *Londonderry Sentinel* was one of the first to employ a photographer. In the 1960s the *Derry Journal* and the Donegal papers had a photographer and many images from that period are included in this collection.

Between 1867 and 1939 there were thirty-one commercial photographers listed in the town directories for Donegal. For most of them, it was a part-time occupation. Stephen Butler of Carndonagh (1876–1959), for example, is also listed as a 'publican and cycle agent' between 1920 and 1939. Some of the images in this collection were purchased by the author from Butler's shop in the 1970s, while others have been supplied by Joseph Butler. The thirty other photographers in the county up to 1939 were J. Benson, Donegal (1913–15); J.D. Cassidy, Ardara (1913); Allen Coon, Letterkenny (1902–38); G. Crowder, Bundoran (1867–1922); P. Devlin, Donegal (1910–17); J.J. Gillespie, Killybegs (1939); F. Harkin, Donegal (1932); Hudson and Benson, Ballybofey (1911); Miss Kelly, Ballyshannon (1939); D. Knox, Dunfanaghy (1890); G. Laidlaw, Lifford (1868–92); Mrs Lawless, Rathmullan (1939); T. McConnell, Ramelton (1890); E. McCosker, Raphoe (1892–1906); P. McCosker, Raphoe (1910–20); McCosker Bros, Raphoe (1907–9); J. McLaughlin, Bundoran (1911–22); Miss Miller and W. Miller, both of Ballyshannon (1913); L. Mulhern, Raphoe (1913); A. Orr, Ramelton (1886–9); J. Pratt, Letterkenny (1870); Revlin, Donegal (1910–15); T.A. Robinson, Donegal (1910–22); W.S. Semple, Manorcunningham (1899); R.G. Simmons, Letterkenny (1881); P. Smyth, Ballyshannon (1868); F. Thompson, Bundoran (1911–16) and W. Watson, Donegal (1877–1939).

The introduction of stereoscopic techniques popularised photography in drawing-rooms in large country houses in the 1880s. Twin images were made on each negative and when printed and viewed through a stereoscope the images blended into one. Such photographs are rare, but this collection includes a previously unpublished stereoscopic image of Terryrone National School in Inishowen (see p. 57).

Schools provided a good source of employment for photographers and three school group photographs from the 1880s can be seen in this book. The development of photography in the county, however, was at a relatively slow pace. In *Thom's Trade Directory* for 1957 there are no photographers listed for Letterkenny, the largest town. There were, of course, large numbers of amateur photographers but their work has not been documented, by and large, although there are some examples in regional publications such as David Martin's book on Killybegs. The late James Canavan of Moville worked in still and cine images for over fifty years from the late 1940s, providing a rich record of events in rural Donegal. International photographers have visited Donegal on a regular basis and the images by Dorothy Harrison Thurman, Martine Franck, Jan Voster and Rachel Geise are well known. Professional photographers worked for the tourist industry, producing postcards for Valentines.

Both Easons and John Hinde have provided a rich harvest of images that have contributed to Donegal's high ranking as a holiday destination. Lithographs backed on linen were printed by W. Colhoun in 1905 for the Donegal Railways, and these colourful images of dramatic landscapes are now quite rare and valuable. Two visitors in particular have supplied many of the images in this publication. A Dutch priest, Father Anthony van der Elsen, has been taking photographs here since the 1960s, while Michael Davies provided some fine pictures of Tory in the 1950s, which are published here for the first time. The Donegal County Council Archives section is in the process of building an interesting collection of images, some of which also appear in this book.

Throughout the nineteenth century the administrative affairs of Donegal were in the hands of the gentlemen of the Grand Jury. They were responsible for a range of functions such as the building and maintenance of roads and bridges, and the management of courthouses, gaols, the infirmary at Lifford and the asylum in Letterkenny; they were also responsible for the payment of officials. Their total budget in 1845 was £32,964 and they were an unelected body. Accusations of fraud were often made against them even by members of their own class and they were regularly accused of favouring their own members in the awarding of contracts for such items as road maintenance. The day-to-day business of running the county was in the hands of the Board of Guardians, whose main function was the running of the workhouses, although they had additional powers of raising local finances.

The Grand Jury mainly comprised wealthy landowners, and the Hamiltons of Brownhall near Ballintra were typical members. Major James Hamilton and his son Captain John Hamilton both feature in a photograph of the Grand Jury at its very last meeting in Lifford in 1899; in that year it was abolished and replaced by the County Council, whose members were elected by residents of the county. John Hamilton was one of three members of the old Grand Jury who was entitled to sit in the new County Council, so he enjoyed the distinction of serving on both bodies. By the second half of the nineteenth century the Hamiltons owned 8,500 acres and

Children at play on their holidays in Donegal in the 1950s. *(McClintock Collection)*

Greencastle Pier, 1970s. *(van der Elsen/Beattie Collection)*

The de Burgo castle, built in 1305 to provide a base for Norman power in the north-west. The Castle Inn is on the right. *(van der Elsen/Beattie Collection)*

today Brownhall is still managed by members of the family. Their history has been recorded by Captain John Hamilton in *My Times and Other Times*, which includes a photograph of eighty-year-old John Hamilton making hay on the family estate. He was the last surviving member of the old Grand Jury living in the county.

As landlords were keen to develop their estates, many of them were closely associated with the growth of towns and villages in the county in the nineteenth century. The Plantation in the seventeenth century had designated certain places as corporate towns and commercial centres where fairs and markets would be held. Among them were Lifford, Donegal, Ballyshannon, Killybegs, Raphoe, Rathmullan and St Johnston. Patents to hold markets were again issued in the eighteenth century and places which received patents included Stranorlar, Ardara, Malin, Killygordon, Ballindrait and Churchill.

There are many examples of landlords showing enterprise and initiative which contributed greatly to the development of a town. In Buncrana, George Vaughan can be regarded as a model of an enterprising landlord, although his efforts did not meet with general approval locally. He built an imposing residence (see p. 50) and drew up plans for the main street which was linked to his home by tree-lined avenues offering impressive views of Lough Swilly and the Fanad peninsula. Realising that the two rivers in the town could provide water power he established a textile mill which attracted the attention of distinguished writers and travellers of the period. To provide workers for his mill he established a training facility for young apprentices: the so-called 'college of weavers'. He also encouraged good farming practices and promoted the growing of flax to supply the raw material for the town's new industry. His methods bore fruit and during periods when harvests failed he was able to supply shiploads of corn from Buncrana to Derry to help relieve the hunger.

Letterkenny established itself as an important market town during the nineteenth century, its success helped by its access to a port on Lough Swilly and the growth of the railway network. Farmers came in from the surrounding districts to sell their produce, such as barley, oats, linen yarn and cloth. It became part of a network of towns that were well established by 1850 as centres for fairs and markets but which also provided employment in the shirt-making industry, as well as in knitting, embroidery, spinning and weaving.

The expansion of government services also helped to consolidate town development. Workhouses and police barracks were built in Carndonagh, Ballyshannon, Dunfanaghy, Donegal, Glenties, Letterkenny, Milford and Stranorlar. The building of hospitals, courthouses, dispensaries, schools and churches all helped in the growth of towns in the county. Other towns developed their own resources, and places like Moville, Bundoran, Buncrana and various small villages on the west coast such as Bunbeg gained a reputation in pre-Famine times as popular bathing places which attracted visitors from larger urban areas such as Derry and Enniskillen. Because of its location Ballyshannon was an important garrison town,

Threshing day in north Donegal, 1980s. *(Beattie Collection)*

while Ardara and Glenties both built up a reputation for textiles. In Rosapenna and Downings Lord Leitrim saw the potential for tourism and provided a hotel, a golf course and public transport for visitors.

But if the tide was rising, it did not lift all boats. Rural areas, particularly in west Donegal, suffered because of poor infrastructure, small uneconomic farms, distance from established markets and the subdivision of holdings among family members. In large families seasonal migration to Scotland or emigration to England and America helped to ease the problems, while for others the hiring fair offered a possible source of income. Hiring fairs called 'Rabbles' were held twice yearly. In Letterkenny they took place on 12 May and 12 November. Children from the age of fourteen came from places such as the Rosses, Falcarragh and Creeslough to seek work on the large farms of the Laggan in central Donegal and in neighbouring counties. Contracts were offered for six months; board and lodgings were provided and a sum of around £12 was paid for the six-month season. A writer called Micí McGowan has left a vivid account of how he was hired at the age of nine in his autobiography, *The Hard Road to the Klondyke*. The fairs petered out in the early 1940s and today the only reminder of those days of hardship is the monument in the Market Square in Letterkenny, depicting a small group of young children waiting to be hired.

By the end of the nineteenth century the British government was hoping to find a solution to the Irish question by introducing Home Rule and land reform. Donegal was in the forefront of the land campaign that culminated in the Land War of the 1880s, in which a Derrybeg priest, Father McFadden, played a prominent role. A series of Land Acts succeeded in bringing agrarian agitation to an end, and one of them in particular (in 1891) had a dramatic effect on the infrastructure of the county. It set up a body called the Congested Districts Board, which covered most of Donegal, and aimed to improve conditions through education, training, new industry, communications and marketing. When the Board ceased to function thirty-two years later it had a considerable list of achievements to its credit, built on a model of community enterprise and rural development. It recognised the importance of fishing to the economy and employed Scottish fishermen to train young men in modern fishing methods using a new type of boat called a 'Zulu'. Over a twenty-year period it provided over 180 boats with nets to fishermen along the Donegal coast to catch the great shoals of herring. A model fishing port was set up in Teelin and boat-building was established at Killybegs. Fish processing was introduced and the new railway network provided quick access to new markets. Thus were laid the foundations of Donegal's pre-eminence in the fishing industry.

The board had other notable achievements but only a few are referred to here. A large weaving school and depot were established at Ardara; co-operative banks were introduced to places as far apart as Bruckless, Cloughaneely and Glenswilly; Downings and Teelin had cooperages; there was a new creamery in Ramelton; a boat-building yard and a carpet factory were set up in Killybegs. Large estates were broken up and land was divided among smallholders; one of the largest was the Musgrave estate of 48,594 acres in south Donegal. Education and vocational training were seen as vital to help small communities survive. A crochet class was started in the small village of Carrowmena in Inishowen, while in Ardara lace-

The re-building of Grianán of Aileach. This rare photograph from 1878 shows the official re-opening of Grianán of Aileach following its reconstruction under the direction of Dr Walter Bernard of Derry (see p. 142). He based his design on surveys drawn up by Petrie (1835), Colby (1837) and Godwin (1858), all of whom reported that it was in a very dilapidated state. With no state aid, he started to rebuild the fort in the spring of 1874, assisted by more than forty local people working one day per week on a voluntary basis. He experienced most difficulty in the reconstruction of the western end; in 2003 similar problems were encountered when this section had to be rebuilt because part of the structure here had collapsed. Although situated in Donegal, the fort is within walking distance of Derry and has been a popular site with visitors for many generations. It commands excellent views, situated as it is 802 feet above sea-level. *(Bigger/McDonald Collection)*

making classes were organised for young women. Parish councils were set up in places like Clonmany and agricultural shows were revived. A fish-curing station was established on the remote island of Inistrahull, off Malin Head.

The creation of the Border in 1922 initially had a negative impact on the economic and social life of the county, impeding the free flow of goods to traditional markets like Derry, Strabane, Coleraine and Enniskillen. In the 1930s the Economic War created enormous difficulties for many small industries and farmers, but for many others life continued as usual. Members of the Derry Garrison Drag Hunt continued to hold their meets in Donegal, accompanied by local farmers; pictures of the hunt can be seen in this book (see p. 137). One of the unexpected consequences of partition was the emergence of a new type of market created by smugglers who found a ready trade for their contraband cigarettes, groceries and farm produce. On a lighter note, this industry generated a whole range of folk tales, myths and legends as the smugglers sought to outwit the zealous members of the excise department of the state.

For years the symbols of the revenue authorities were dotted along the Border between Derry, Tyrone and Fermanagh in a dreary display of green and grey temporary customs posts. It seemed they were destined to remain for ever but the advent of the European Economic Community in 1973 led eventually to the closure of the posts and this provided a boost for cross-Border trade. Cooperation of a cross-Border nature received a further impetus with the signing of the Good Friday Agreement in 1998. It has not been a one-way process, and Donegal people have taken full advantage of the opportunities offered in business, marketing, third-level education, cultural heritage and social life. In fact many of the images in this collection have taken on a cross-Border life of their own, reflecting the myriad ways in which Donegal people have endeavoured to live in harmony with their neighbours.

St Patrick's Memorial Church of the Four Masters, Donegal Town. The building was opened on 17 March 1935 by Bishop McNeely, who described it as a great Celtic church with its lofty round tower and high pointed roofs. It is regarded as a classic of modern Irish ecclesiastical architecture. The architects were Byrne & Sons of Dublin. It was seen at the time as a triumph for Irish craftsmen, who used native materials: granite from Barnesmore and the Rosses; sandstone from Mountcharles and Drimkeelan; slates from the quarries at St Johnston; oak and marble from Connemara and Cork. Among those who subscribed to the new church were John Keeny, a Donegal man from Philadelphia and S.M. Gallagher, a local solicitor. The contractors were Donnelly & Sons. (*Jim Gallagher*)

1

Highways and Byways: Towns and Villages

View of Letterkenny from Leck

This chapter serves to illustrate the slogan used in tourism advertising, 'Up here, it's different.' The coastline, with its rugged cliffs and sandy beaches, contrasts with the hills, valleys and mountains of the interior. Every town and village is undergoing rapid change, with the population of some places almost doubling in size in the last ten years. There is a strong contrast between the images presented here and the county today. Over half a century ago there were cattle fairs in most country towns and farm produce was marketed by smallholders in the town square just as it had been when the markets were established in the seventeenth century by enterprising landlords. There were very few cars parked in the streets; small shops were more plentiful and traditional shop signs were evident; the pace of life was much slower.

The Donegal historian A.G. Lecky described the physical structure of the county as saucer-shaped with a hilly, outer rim and a flat, fertile interior. Territorial units were originally protected by powerful chieftains and the word *cenel* was used to describe the place belonging to a particular ruling family. From the fifth century the 'Cenel Chonaill', a powerful family unit led by Conall, ruled most of the county. Donegal was later divided into baronies, and subsequently into rural and urban districts. Today there are geographical divisions, such as the Irish-speaking Rosses, the central plain of the Laggan, the Bluestacks and Magh Eine; other districts are associated with the rivers, headlands and inlets that neighbour them. Two passes, Barnesmore and Glengesh, provide access between the north and the south.

For over a century the county has been famous for its cloth and Donegal homespun tweed enjoys a worldwide reputation. The industry started out in the nineteenth century with humble spinners and weavers working in dimly lit thatched cottages. In the period from 1891 to 1923 the Congested Districts Board transformed the industry, setting up lace and crochet schools, providing looms, helping to set up the Killybegs carpet factory and training craftworkers to market their products. Ardara became a centre for the tweed industry in the county.

Deep-water ports and harbours feature prominently in the images presented here because of the importance of the fishing industry. It is striking to note the number of punts, drontheims and steamers that crowded into the harbours in the 1920s when the herring industry was at its peak. In places like Killybegs, Greencastle, Burtonport and Teelin fishing was the main source of income.

Some of Donegal's towns have an exciting architectural heritage and Ramelton, Rathmullan, Raphoe and Ballyshannon are foremost among them. Squares and diamonds used for open markets are to be found in Letterkenny, Donegal Town, Malin, Buncrana and Moville. Holiday resorts such as Bundoran, Rossnowlagh, Rosapenna, Downings, Dunfanaghy, Bunbeg and Dungloe have been attracting visitors since the early 1800s.

Literary figures have helped other places to win recognition. Mountcharles produced Seamus McManus; Paddy MacGill is remembered at the Glenties Summer School; a Clonmany weaver, Charles McGlinchey, is celebrated at the McGlinchey School; playwright Charles Macklin is honoured at the Autumn School in Culdaff; Frank McGuinness comes from Buncrana; Brian Friel lives in Greencastle; Cathal Ó Searcaigh is our best-known Irish language poet. Lough Derg near Pettigo is a place of reflection and penance. Gartan and Kilmacrennan are associated with Colmcille, and the Franciscans' long association with the county is evident at Rossnowlagh. In the west the Irish language can be heard in the streets of Falcarragh, Gortahork and Derrybeg. The images in this chapter show a county with a colourful past that is undergoing constant change.

ain Street, Ballyshannon, *c.* 1900. The Imperial Hotel is on the right, next to the grocery shop of obert Anderson, whose wedding photo appears on p. 134. At the foot of the town is the Belfast anking Company building, which was constructed in 1878 and has an attractive clock-tower. Nearby as the house of William Connolly, who was elected Speaker of the Irish House of Commons in 1715. 1911 the street was a thriving commercial centre with at least eight grocery shops, five drapery ores, three spirit merchants, a watchmaker and a dressmaker. The next street was Castle Street, and ne of the grocery shops was Lipsetts. The family lived above the shop and the children all helped in e business. Sally Lipsett became a schoolteacher and married George Corscadden, a member of a well-nown local farming family. They settled in Scotland, where George owned several butcher's shops, and ey lived at 312 Dennison Gardens in Glasgow. In 1923 Sally was home on holiday when her second ild was born on 12 June above Lipsett's shop. The baby was christened Hazel and she was baptised the nearby Protestant Church of St Anne's three months later on 24 September 1923. Young Hazel ent back to Glasgow with her parents. As a young woman she found work as a typist and married clerk called Leo Blair. Their son Tony became Prime Minister, thus providing Ballyshannon with a cond link to the House of Commons. *(Ulster Museum)*

Donegal from the air, photographed by Captain Morgan, September 1954. In March 1612 Basil Brooke, who was granted lands in Donegal, agreed to build a town on the River Eske, with a marketplace, a church, cottages and a school. He took over the castle, formerly the headquarters of the O'Donnells, and refurbished it. The banqueting room contains an ornate fireplace with his family crest. The castle is now open to the public. The Diamond has an obelisk dedicated to the Four Masters, who wrote the *Annals of the Kingdom of Ireland up to 1616*. Donegal town is a popular gateway to the county for visitors. Places to see include the site of the old Franciscan friary, dating back to 1474; the castle; Magee's, a shop founded in 1866 and famous for its tweeds; the Craft Village; and Donegal's most attractive bookshop, the Four Masters. *(National Library of Ireland)*

Bundoran on the rocks, *c.* 1950. With the town of Bundoran as a backdrop, a group of gentlemen take their greyhounds for a walk. When the naturalist Lloyd Praeger visited Bundoran in the 1930s, he wrote that he was impressed by the rock-pools in the level beds of limestone, a landscape similar to the one seen here. *(Bigger/McDonald Collection)*

The Imperial Hotel, Bundoran, 1940s. The Irish Tourist Authority's Official Guide of the time recommended bathing at Horse Pool Cove and at Rogay Pool which has a high-diving platform. Other attractions include golf, boating, tennis on the Promenade Courts and amusement fairs on the Promenade. Anglers are catered for at Lough Melvin, the Drowes River and the Benduff River. Enthusiasts can play billiards at the Marine Hotel and Gaelic football in Bayview Avenue. In her 1940s advertisement Miss M. Flanigan promised 'courteous service', but even in the early 1960s, cheques were not accepted in payment of accounts. *(Bigger/McDonald Collection)*

The Allingham Hotel, Bundoran, in the 1940s. The hotel is named after the nineteenth-century poet William Allingham, who was born at the Mall in Ballyshannon and spent most of his life in London. He was a friend of various literary greats including Alfred, Lord Tennyson and Thomas Carlyle. Between 1850 and 1887 he wrote twelve volumes of verse. His leisure time was often spent in Bundoran. He died in 1889 and is buried in St Anne's churchyard, which overlooks the town. *(Bigger/McDonald Collection)*

Refreshment rooms, Bundoran, in the 1950s. Popularly known as 'The Tearooms', and situated at the railway station, this was a familiar sight to the thousands of people who flocked to this tourist resort by train every summer. The town's population of 1,413 in the 1950s increased several times over during the summer season when the Great Northern Railway Company brought tourists to the town. The Tearooms have since been demolished and the new council offices have been built close by. *(Bigger/McDonald Collection)*

Bundoran in the 1930s. The Hamilton Hotel is on the right, with the original Holyrood Hotel above. In the 1960s the hotel's proprietor, J. McEniff, offered guests the comfort of an all-weather veranda. McCloy's grocery is advertised on a gable wall. The shop also sold souvenirs, cutlery, glassware, electroplated goods, china, delft, jewellery, fancy goods, smokers' requisites and stationery. *(Bigger/McDonald Collection)*

Bundoran, late 1930s. Master Daly's Tourist Hotel is on the left, next to Brennan's Criterion Bar, which has been in the family for over a century. Their motto is 'Come as a Stranger, Leave as a Friend'. Next is Cleary's, with Hamilton's Bar at the corner of Railway Road. Note the two water pumps, one of which is outside Brennan's. On the right is P. McDonnell's shop advertising Players' and Wills' cigarettes. The third poster appears to be a newspaper offering 'All of the Big Fight in Pictures'. Kelly's Ocean Bar is next to Wynn's tailors, followed by McPhillip's Shell House, which is still covered in the original sea-shells added to the building by a previous owner who collected them from local beaches. The first ice cream cones were sold in this shop but Crowders also sold ice cream. Other shops included Carroll's, Hamilton's/Kelly's and Renison's grocers. *(National Library of Ireland)*

Waiting for the hunt, 1930s. Hunt supporters wait outside McLaughlin's Bar in Newtowncunningham for the Derry Garrison Drag Hunt to arrive. In a drag hunt the hounds follow a scent laid down on a pre-arranged route across the countryside. No animals are hunted. Soldiers from the garrison usually took their horses across the Border during the night so that they were ready for the hunt the next day. Local residents such as Major Denaro often joined in, as did many farmers. The hunt season ended on St Patrick's Day with point-to-point races at Carricklea near Strabane. *(Bigger/McDonald Collection)*

entral Hotel, Bundoran. The original hotel was built over a century ago. In 1908 the travel writer lgar Shrubsole noted that it had 'electric light throughout' and that there were 'ample supplies' of trol for visitors. It was erected by Robert Sweeney, a Ballyshannon businessman, and the Cassidy mily were among its subsequent owners. Éamon de Valera was a patron of the hotel. It was destroyed fire in 1979 and a new building has since been constructed on the site. *(Bigger/McDonald Collection)*

The Hamilton Hotel, Bundoran. The hotel was a landmark at the foot of the town and is now part of the Hollyrood Hotel. In the 1940s the Irish Tourist Authority's guide urged anglers to contact Mr N.C. Hamilton of the Hamilton Hotel if they wished to fish on the River Drowse, which it described as one of the earliest salmon fisheries in Ireland, with the season opening on the first day of January. Guests had access to a private shooting and fishing demesne. *(Bigger/McDonald Collection)*

This traditional cottage in Inishowen is thatched with locally grown flax or 'lint', as it was called. Wooden pegs attached to the wall are used to secure the ropes covering the thatch. To help retain heat in the cottage there is no back door. There are two rooms and on the right is the 'outshot', which projected out about two feet to accommodate a double bed beside the fireplace in the kitchen. The roof timbers were made of bog oak recovered from local bogs and a layer of heather was used as insulation. Many of these cottages are over two hundred years old but they are slowly disappearing from the landscape. *(van der Elsen/Beattie Collection)*

Killybegs pier, early 1900s. The Congested Districts Board gave a grant towards the building of the Steamboat Pier which cost £10,000 and was completed in 1897. It differed from most other piers on the coast in that it was built of wood. It was expected that it would serve passenger ships sailing to America. The boat seen here was probably provided by the Congested Districts Board which had introduced a new type of boat called a Zulu, which had a large sail. The railway to Killybegs was completed in 1893 and an extension to the pier was added so that fish could be loaded directly onto the train for onward transportation to markets throughout the country. New fish markets were opened up in Belfast and Manchester. In the late 1890s Scottish merchants came to the Rosses and began exporting salted herring. Curing stations were set up along the coast at Inistrahull Island, Downings, Tory Island, Malinbeg and Teelin. The old pier was replaced in the 1950s. The large three-storey building to the right is Gannon's Hotel. On the left are small grocery shops. St Mary's Church, which dates from the 1840s, overlooks the town. Today, Killybegs is one of the country's most important fishing ports. (*Eason Collection/National Library of Ireland*)

Rogers Hotel and shop, Killybegs, in the 1920s or early 1930s. Lyons Tea and a brand of porridge flakes are advertised on the shop front. There was also a post office on the premises. Sheridan & Co. owned the drapery shop on the left; this was originally the Royal Bay View Hotel. Further down the street on the right is Rogers motor garage, while on the left is John Ward's shop. Rogers Hotel has now been replaced by the Bayview Hotel. *(National Library of Ireland)*

Burtonport quay and pier. The fishing industry at Burtonport was boosted in 1783 when Burton Conyngham received a grant of £30,000 to establish a herring industry, which collapsed because of inadequate marketing. A century later fishing began to recover when the Congested Districts Board came to the rescue, setting up a cooperage in Burtonport in the 1890s and a curing station nearby. A local priest, Fr Bernard Walker, helped to get two boats fitted out. Work for both men and women was also available at the kippering station on Edernish Island. *(Beattie Collection)*

The Tourist Hotel and Tourist Restaurant, bearing the words Tourist Lodge over the door, were landmarks for many years in the centre of Bundoran. Both were owned by the schoolteacher and councillor Master Daly, who used one of the buildings as his office. The Tourist Lodge is still standing but the Hotel has been demolished. *(Bigger McDonald Collection)*

ungloe achieved some recognition as a market town in the nineteenth century, with visitors describing s bustling, noisy market, but it was the success of Paddy 'the Cope' Gallagher in establishing a form of ommunity self-help that attracted attention in the twentieth century. The Templecrone Co-operative ociety aimed to supply agricultural products to struggling farmers who were at the mercy of local aders and it became a model of community enterprise for other rural areas. Today the annual 'Mary om Dungloe' festival attracts thousands of visitors and is one of the most successful events of its kind the county. *(Beattie Collection)*

lenties Fair Day, *c.* 1900. The fair was held on the 12th of each month, with markets on Mondays. airs were central to the rural economy. It was estimated by the Congested Districts Board in 1892 that family of six in this area had an annual income of £28. This was based on the price of a cow at £5 nd a sheep at 14*s*. Other income came from the sale of eggs, a pig, butter and webs of cloth. Eggs were enerally bartered and credit was frequently used, especially during the spring before farm produce was vailable to sell at the market. With the arrival of the railway, cattle were loaded into wagons and taken the port at Derry for export. *(Lawrence Collection/National Library of Ireland)*

Hegarty's Hotel, one of the oldest hotels in the county, shown here in the 1940s, stood opposite th Market Square in Letterkenny. An advertisement of 1893 states that it had been established for ove eighty years and that the owner was Mrs Peoples. Like so many of the town's fine landmarks, it ha since been demolished to make way for one of the town's many shopping complexes. It was listed in th *Commercial Directory* for the town in the 1950s. In an age when deliveries were still carried out by hors and cart, one motor car can be seen to the left. *(Bigger/McDonald Collection)*

Three gentlemen stand outside a chemist's shop in Upper Main Street, Letterkenny, 1940s. This shop was originally owned by Tedley Moore, who was richly praised in Canon Maguire's *History of the Diocese of Raphoe* (1920) for his service to the community over forty years. A veterinary surgeon, Tom McClintock (left), later took over the shop as a veterinary chemist's. In 1921 the name 'Moore and Co.' could still be seen over the door but by the time this photograph wa taken it had been replaced b the word 'Chemist'. The sho stood next door to a hotel which was demolished in 2004. *(McClintock Collection*

A lively scene in Letterkenny on Fair Day as a 'trick o'the loop man' entertains young and old, *c.* 1950, by balancing three glasses on a spoon. A fraudster was often described as a 'trick 'o' the loop' man. (*McClintock Collection*)

Benson's sale, *c.* 1925. The bold advertising for Benson's Great Clearance Sale was designed to catch the eye. The shop in Main Street in Letterkenny was originally a drapery store owned by the Magee Brothers, and the name of their firm can still be seen in red lettering on the black tiles at the entrance to Speer's drapery shop in Lower Main Street in the town and also on the interior glass entrance doors. Typical of shops of the period, clothing was hung outside and in the doorway to attract shoppers. James Benson, from Five-Mile-Town, Co Tyrone, retired in 1955 when Ernest Speer took over as draper and outfitter. (*McClintock Collection*)

The large crowd at the unveiling of the statue of Cardinal O'Donnell in the grounds of St Eunan's Cathedral, Letterkenny. A native of Kilraine in Glenties, he was born in 1855 and attended the Old Seminary in the town. He died in 1927. The ceremony was conducted by Professor of Theology Fr Michael O'Donnell, a relation who bears a striking resemblance to the Cardinal. The picture was taken by a niece of Dr O'Donnell. Sculpted by Francis Doyle, the statue was made in the London foundry of Morris-Stringer in 1929. (McClintock Collection)

Sam Fleming, pictured outside his farmhouse at Windyhall, north of Letterkenny, c. 1970. His grandfather, a native of Limavady, was well known in the town as a flax buyer and cattle farmer, who also had a milk round. Sam was a founder member of the Young Farmers' Clubs and the National Farmers' Association. A keen historian, he also wrote a short history of Letterkenny and contributed an article about the Dill family to the *Journal of the County Donegal Historical Society.* *(McClintock Collection)*

The chemist's shop in Letterkenny has been renamed the Medical Stores in this photograph of about 1940. The tradition of roadworks in the main street has a long history although at this time of course the work was entirely manual. *(McClintock Collection)*

'he Kelso Wedding from Letterkenny', 1890. This group picture was taken by the Kerr studio in Derry.
Bigger/McDonald Collection)

Main Street, Stranorlar, 1950s. Thomas 'Dilly' Gillespie enjoying the sunshine outside his shop, now a private residence. The house next door, Whitelaws, with its ornate doorway, has since been demolished; an Ordnance Survey benchmark stone from the 1830s has disappeared. The projecting porch belongs to the hotel, which Willie Kee purchased in 1892. Further up the street, out of view, is Raitt's hardware store, which had a courthouse upstairs, with a chemist's shop next door. The Band Field, where British Army regiments entertained the townsfolk, was behind Raitt's. McNulty's butcher's shop is on the left. The whitewashed wall remains but the neighbouring bungalow has gone. Partially visible is Thompson's thatched cottage, since demolished. *(Ulster Museum)*

The Congested Districts Board set up a weaving school and a tweed depot in Ardara, thus laying th foundations for the town's tweed industry. To ensure the webs were of high quality, a bonus was paid i they reached a given standard. A County Down textile manufacturer, W.T.D. Walker, was in charge an he opened centres at Carrick and Milford. The lace-makers are pictured here outside the embroidery dep in 1900. They are dressed in some style, with clean white smocks serving as aprons and boots, whic were normally reserved for social occasions. The photographer was Robert Welsh, who worked for th Congested Districts Board. On his visit to Ardara he was accompanied by a businessman, Henry Hamilto of the 'White House', Portrush, who was interested in purchasing tweed cloth. *(Ulster Museum)*

This postcard view of Glenties, *c.* 1950, comes from the studio of S.R. Butler of Carndonagh, who travelled all over the county taking pictures of the main towns. Only half a dozen cars are parked in the street. Today Glenties is renowned for winning several Tidy Town awards. Brian Friel's mother lived here and the film *Dancing at Lúghnasa* was based on her family. The annual MacGill Summer School has also become an important feature of life in the town. *(Beattie Collection)*

The Stewart Arms in Dunfanaghy, early 1900s. It is now known as the Carraig Rua Hotel. The Stewarts of Ards were local landlords, who had bought the estate from William Wray in 1782. Guidebooks of the 1950s promoted golf as a major attraction for tourists. The 18-hole course here was 5,280 yards long and green fees were 2s per day. The Secretary was W.T. Arnold and guests were reminded that Sunday play was permitted. A promotion by Arnold's Hotel noted that milk, poultry and vegetables were produced on the hotel farm. *(Bigger/McDonald Collection)*

Rosapenna Hotel in the Rosguill peninsula, *c.* 1900. Construction was started by the 4th Earl of Leitrim in 1892 in order to develop tourism. The hotel was built of wood imported from Sweden. A steamship service was established between Mulroy in North Donegal and Scotland to improve access for visitors. It was also possible to travel by train from Derry to Fahan, and then take the ferry to Rathmullan; the hotel provided a coach and horses to take passengers to their destination. The 5th Earl supplied the hotel with farm produce and even introduced a bus service from Strabane to Rosapenna. Robert Welsh the photographer was a frequent visitor and along with other clients spent much of his time on the veranda, which he greatly admired. *(Ulster Museum)*

Opposite: Rosapenna guests enjoying the fine views of the Donegal landscape. *(Ulster Museum)*

A quiet street scene in Milford, *c.* 1940. On the right is the chemist's shop belonging to Owen McCormick MPSI, who is described as a dispensing chemist. This shop was opened in January 1936 and is still run by the McCormicks. A few doors further up is the Court House, built in 1884 by Robert Clements, 4th Earl of Leitrim. His predecessor, William Sidney Clements, was assassinated in 1878. Robert was a popular landlord; he also built the Market House, a town hall and a corn mill, and started a steamship service between Milford and Glasgow to encourage trade and tourism. In the Irish Free State's *Official Handbook* (1932) the Milford Hotel is described as 'what an Angler's Hotel should be'. *(Bigger/McDonald Collection)*

The thatched Doe Church near Creeslough was built in 1784 (before the granting of Emancipation) and was one of the oldest churches in use in the Diocese of Raphoe. The site was donated by members of the Wray family who were the landlords. In the *Ordnance Survey Memoirs*, it is recorded that in 1834 there were only two public buildings in the area, the parish church and the Roman Catholic chapel. The church was closed in 1971 and later demolished when the new church of St Michael at Creeslough was built. The bell-tower can be seen to the left. It was built in 1918 and Michael O'Callaghan of Letterkenny was the architect. The parochial house can also be seen. The new church at Creeslough opened in 1971. It was designed by the award-winning architect Liam McCormick of Greencastle, who also designed Burt Church and many other churches throughout Ireland. The design is based on the main feature on the landscape, Muckish mountain. This postcard is from the studio of S.R. Butler, Carndonagh. *(Joseph Butler)*

Opposite: Milford Church near Mulroy Bay was opened in 1860 and served a Church of Ireland congregation. It was in the ancient parish of Tullyfern which included parts of Kilmacrenan and Tullyaughnish. On 7 October 1982 it was struck by lightning and badly damaged, and was later demolished. Only a portion of the porch remains. The parish is now united with Tullyaughnish. *(Bigger/McDonald Collection)*

Rathmullan bus, 1960s. After the closure of the railway, the Lough Swilly bus service provided public transport for the county. Bus no. 91, an Albion Nimbus, was purchased in 1958 in the second of two batches of three. These were the last new buses the company bought. The timber-framed body was built by O'Doherty & Co. of Strabane and Lifford, who built tail-car trailers for the County Donegal Railways. The passengers are boarding the bus in Rathmullan, although the destination is Letterkenny via Burt. The postman is Tommy Carr. A Ford Anglia can be seen to the left. The Swilly is to the right of the low wall and embankment. *(Anthony Moyes)*

Kilmacrennan has close associations with the Irish missionary Colmcille (521–97), who spent his youth here tutored by Cruithneachan. The Friary has links with the Franciscans and Manus O'Donnell the Irish chieftain. Bishop Patrick McGettigan was born here in 1785. In 1834 the Revd Anthony Hastings noted in the *Ordnance Survey Memoirs* that residents here spoke English with a Scottish accent a reminder of the Plantation. In this photograph from the early 1900s Coyle's drapery shop is on the corner. Opposite on the left is Hogan's dressmakers and McCafferty's pub. The thatched house is Duffy's tearooms, popular with Doon Well pilgrims. The initials SB over the arched gateway are those of Sam Burns, with Stewart's tearooms next door. *(National Library of Ireland)*

Burt landscape, late 1970s. This dramatic view overlooks the land reclaimed by Dr McDonald, an English industrialist who brought the Birmingham Sound Reproducers factory to Derry. Inch Lake, a noted bird sanctuary, can be seen, as can the Embankment. On Inch Island archaeologists have recently excavated a number of coastal habitation sites dating back to the Mesolithic period. The Lough Swilly ferry was revived in May 2004 and now provides transport across the lough between Buncrana's new pier and Rathmullan. Inishowen can be seen on the right and the Fanad peninsula on the left. *(van der Elsen/Beattie Collection)*

Buncrana, *c.* 1960. There are two pubs on the left, Hutton's and Hegarty's. The sign for the Central Restaurant is also visible. On the right is Grant's bar. At the top of the street the flat-roofed modern structure Castle Buildings, with Rose O'Connor's grocery shop and the Castle café next door. *(Beattie Collection)*

The Square, Moville, 1940s. A group of chemists from Northern Ireland had taken a day trip to Moville in two Lough Swilly buses. McKinney's Hotel (now the Foyle Hotel) is on the right; the building next door bears the words 'Lough Swilly Transport' and was known locally as the Depot. Today it is a bookshop and newspaper outlet. Further up the street stands the Co-operative Society store and Sam Cooke's grocery shop, now under new management. On the left the awning bears the words 'Crumlish – Butcher's Shop'. An Esso oil lorry can be seen behind the pole. *(Bigger/McDonald Collection)*

Carndonagh, 1930s. A solitary motor car heads towards Malin. The bar on the left is the New Century Bar, no doubt celebrating the turn of the twentieth century. On the right is Kearney's cottage, which was demolished in the 1990s to make way for the County Council Offices and Public Library. This is the view that greeted train passengers who arrived at the station and headed towards the Diamond. *(Bigger/McDonald Collection)*

2

A Heritage in Stone

This unusual view of the Church of St Aengus at Burt, close to one of Ireland's most historic sites at the Grianán of Aileach, is a fitting opening for this section. Its design combines uniquely the ancient and modern, and it is a fine example of twentieth-century architecture. The building embodies the best in traditional rural stonework and modern architecture. There is a circular theme throughout; even the granite path shown here, leading up from the main road, is laid out in curved patterns. The religious art at the entrance, on a stone screen-wall, is the work of the famous Irish sculptor Oisin Kelly. *(van der Elsen/Beattie Collection)*

The Catholic church at Burt was dedicated in 1967. It was commissioned by Bishop Neil Farren of Derry to reflect twentieth-century changes in liturgy and architecture, and was designed by Liam McCormick, who was awarded the RIAI Triennial Gold Medal in 1971 for his work. Helen Maloney designed the stained glass and the work of the sculptor Imogen Stuart can be seen inside the church. Voted the 'Building of the Century', the church is a landmark on the Derry–Letterkenny road, and is popular with worshippers and visitors alike. *(van der Elsen/Beattie Collection)*

Sacred Heart Church, Carndonagh. Built in 1945, this neo-Romanesque church is situated in an elevated position overlooking the town of Carndonagh. The architect was Ralph Byrne of Dublin. The statues on the dome of the church are by Albert Power. The church has undergone extensive internal renovations recently. The town's main historic feature is the Carndonagh Cross. The Franciscan scholar John Colgan was born outside the town in 1592, and wrote many works on philosophy and religion, including *Acta Sanctorum Hiberniae*. *(Beattie Collection)*

The Border village of Muff, *c.* 1960. McHale's thatched cottage and shop, which have recently been demolished to make way for new shops, are on the right. The gable of the Garda barracks and an Esso petrol sign can be seen in the centre of the picture. On the left, hidden behind the trees, is the Borderland dance-hall, which hosted top bands such as the Royal and the Capitol in the late 1950s. Further north is St Mary's Hall, which was opened as a parish dance-hall in 1955 by Bishop Farren, with the Irish tenor Joseph McNally as the main attraction. Lynch's shirt factory is just out of the picture. *(Bigger/ McDonald Collection)*

Ballyliffin, 1940s. The Ballyliffin Hotel is on the right, while the railway station and railway sheds can be clearly seen in the centre. Roof writing was evidently a popular form of advertising in the 1940s. A group of thatched cottages is visible on the left. Carrickabraghy Castle can just be seen in the distance. Ballyliffin is now better known for its excellent hotels and golf courses. This postcard is from the Butler studio in Carndonagh. *(Beattie Collection)*

Buncrana Castle, 1718. Built by an enterprising landlord, Colonel George Vaughan, the castle is now a private residence. A member of the Grand Jury, Vaughan was largely responsible for the design of the town of Buncrana. He had the main street laid out with elegant driveways, lined with trees, leading to his demesne. He also owned salmon fishing rights to the River Crana. Of his four sisters, three were known in polite circles as the 'Three Graces', and married into some of the leading families of the day, the Harts, the Brookes and the Sampsons. Vaughan also built mills and harnessed the water power of the town's two rivers. He was a great lover of Irish music, particularly the harp, and is known to have welcomed travelling musicians such as the blind harpist John Carraher and given them hospitality, as was the custom in some of the great houses of the period. He also appreciated good literature and built up an extensive private library. The castle caught the attention of visitors to Buncrana such as Bishop Pococke in 1752, who was impressed by its location overlooking Lough Swilly and admired its gardens and plantations. Vaughan died in 1763 and is buried in Fahan graveyard. Although he can be described as the founder of the modern town, his grave is unmarked (although its location is known). Vaughan had no male heirs and after his death the castle passed out of the hands of the Vaughan family. In the 1840s the deputy lieutenant Daniel Todd was registered as the owner. In 1902 the American travel writer Samuel Bayne stayed in the castle as a guest and was highly impressed by the beauty of its gardens. He was touring Donegal by jaunting car and his horses were accommodated in the castle's stables. *(Beattie Collection)*

New Park, photographed by S.R. Butler of Carndonagh, *c.* 1930. New Park, Moville, was the home of the Montgomery family. It was originally built in 1776 by Samuel Montgomery, who also developed Moville itself. Sir Robert Montgomery was born here in 1809. His son became Bishop of Tasmania and his grandson was Field Marshal Montgomery of Alamein, who enjoyed childhood holidays here. For a short period in the 1980s it was a popular hotel, but it is now unoccupied. It has an impressive doorway and a magnificent staircase; the bishop's oratory was upstairs, overlooking the lawns where tennis and croquet were played. His wife Maud was the last member of the family to live here. A tree on which the Montgomerys carved their names has been cut down. *(Beattie Collection)*

Buncrana Mill, shown here in the 1930s, was one of the industrial landmarks of the town, built in 1803 by Crookshank and Kennedy and later known as Wilson's Mill. It reached the peak of production during the Napoleonic Wars when its sail cloth was in heavy demand. The mill was destroyed by fire in 1827 and rebuilt by Samuel Alexander in 1838. At the start of the Famine it employed some two hundred people in flax spinning. Richardsons of Lambeg bought the mill after the Famine but it closed in 1876 although the machinery was maintained for several years afterwards. It was demolished in the 1940 and Harry Swan, a member of a well-known milling family, donated the site to the town of Buncrana a a town park. All that remains of the old mill is part of a wall. *(Bigger/McDonald Collection)*

Situated in the Finn Valley near Ballybofey, Glenmore House is a lavish example of a Georgian country house with a fine courtyard. A century ago it was redesigned in a black-and-white half-timbered Tudor style. In 1876 William Style, a former owner, owned 39,564 acres. He granted a plot for the building of the Protestant church of Kilteevogue nearby, which was opened by Bishop Alexander in 1879. A celebration banquet was held afterwards in Glenmore House. It has recently been partly demolished but the two gate lodges dating from the late 1830s are still standing. *(McClintock Collection)*

Glebe House near Ballybofey was built by the Revd Robert Butt in 1779 and its exterior remains largely unchanged from Butt's time. His son Isaac (1813–79) became a barrister; he defended the Young Irelanders and later became a Member of Parliament for Limerick. He was also President of the Amnesty Association, but he is best known as the leader of the Home Rule Party in Parliament from 1870 to 1879. He is buried in Stranorlar. His monumental contribution to Irish politics has not been given the recognition it deserves. *(Beattie Collection)*

Rathmullan Priory was built by Rory McSweeney in about 1508 for Carmelite monks. During the Nine Years' War it was plundered by George Bingham and was subsequently turned into a barracks by Ralph Bingley in 1601. After the Plantation the nave was converted into a residence by Bishop Knox of Raphoe, whose initials can still be seen over the door. It was used as a parish church until 1814 when it was abandoned. In the graveyard is a memorial to the victims of the *Saldahna*, which sank in Lough Swilly in 1811. The town is now linked to Inishowen by ferry, and visitors can enjoy a fine beach and excellent hotels. The Flight of the Earls Heritage Centre is dedicated to this great historic event of 1607 and is worth a visit. *(Ulster Museum)*

Cloghan Lodge, shown here in the 1940s, was used as a hunting lodge by Sir Charles Style of Glenmore. A generous landlord, he is reputed to have paid the tithes of his tenants. He is listed among the Donegal gentry in *Pigott's Directory* in 1824. Some traditions survive, and hunting and fishing are still available to guests at the lodge today. *(Beattie Collection)*

A woman and a child stand in the shade at Culdaff National School in 1885. This photograph from the Kerr studio is described as 'Miss Campbell's School'. In 1880 the school had its maximum number of pupils, with eighty-seven enrolled. It was a Church of Ireland National School until the middle of the twentieth century and is now a private residence. *(Bigger/ McDonald Collection)*

Thatched cottage near Malin Head, *c.* 1960. This cottage is an example of traditional rural architecture which is now under threat. The roof is held down by ropes and wooden pegs secured to the walls so that it would withstand the strongest of Atlantic gales. The door is typically in the centre, although this house lacks the traditional storm-porch associated with this area. The shed attached to it was used as a byre and barn, and its chimney indicates that it had a fireplace for boiling potatoes which were fed to livestock. The shed's thatch has since been removed and replaced by corrugated tin. *(van der Elsen/Beattie Collection)*

Terryrone National School, *c.* 1882. This stereoscopic photograph has never been published and is the only one in this collection. When the photograph is looked at through a special viewer the two images merge to form an extremely clear picture. The school was located outside Moville, and a new building was erected in 1931. *(Bigger/McDonald Collection)*

The village of Bunbeg, 1912. Situated on the River Clady in Gweedore, the village was built by an enterprising landlord called Lord George Hill, who in 1834 purchased 23,000 acres of land. His activities are described in his book *Facts from Gweedore*. He constructed many of the buildings seen here. The corn shed on the left was built in 1831 and has an Irish inscription over the door. There was also a shop, as well as a school and a grain store. Hill was also responsible for introducing a hotel and setting up a model farm. *(Ulster Museum)*

Swan's Mill, Buncrana, after the 1931 fire. The Swans were millers and the mill at the foot of Lower Main Street was one of the town's main buildings, dating from 1858. For many years it was a major centre of employment. In the 1950s Thomas Swan & Co. Ltd manufactured 'White Swan Flaked Oats', which was advertised as 'Donegal's Best Breakfast'. The packaging bore a drawing of a white swan on Lough Swilly with the Inishowen hills in the background. *(Bigger/McDonald Collection)*

Swan's Mill caught fire at 8pm on 23 March 1931. The North Wing was badly damaged but was rebuilt up to the level of the Centre Block with stones from Barr's quarry at Gransha. The Swan Brothers had brought electricity to the town in 1905. During the fire the power-house was saved and electricity was restored in the town the day after the fire. Gardai and citizens formed a bucket chain to assist the firefighters. Free State soldiers under Captain Tynan and Lieutenant Power helped fight the blaze. The Derry fire brigade also assisted. *(Bigger/McDonald Collection)*

Greenbank Presbyterian Church. This attractive stone structure on the Derry–Moville road has been in use since 1862. The church hall next door, which was built by voluntary labour by the local congregation, was destroyed by fire in 2003. Here a horse and carriage wait outside for a wedding party. *(Beattie Collection)*

Eunan's College was opened in Letterkenny in 1906. It cost £22,000 and took over eighteen months to build. It was constructed at a time when the town was undergoing a massive programme of development. The population of the town in 1901 was 4,361. The school replaced the old Diocesan Seminary which had prepared students for the priesthood. Most of the staff transferred from the seminary to the new school. Dormitories provided accommodation for boarding pupils who came from other parts of the county where secondary education was not available. Built in Irish Romanesque style, the college occupies a dominant position overlooking the town and includes unusual features such as a cloistered courtyard and towers. *(McClintock Collection)*

Franciscans at Ards, *c.* 1950. The Franciscan links with Donegal date back to medieval times. Nuala O'Donnell invited the Order to the county in 1474 and they were very closely associated with the O'Donnell clan for centuries afterwards. They were involved with Hugh O'Neill and Rory O'Donnell in the Flight of the Earls in 1607 and members of the order compiled *The Annals of the Four Masters* in the seventeenth century. In 1946 the order was welcomed back to Donegal and the new Friary was opened at Rossnowlagh. A new church was opened in 1952. *(McClintock Collection)*

Station Island. Pilgrims to Lough Derg are seen here in 1905 taking part in a spiritual exercise at one of the nine stations. The traditional pilgrimage involves three days of fasting and two days of prayer. Pilgrims have specified prayers to say at each station and the exercises are completed barefoot. Here the pilgrim recites one Our Father, one Hail Mary and the Creed. This station is St Patrick's Cross. The stone shaft in which the cross is set dates back to the Middle Ages and is a relic of monastic times on the island. The pilgrimage is still very popular and can be undertaken during the summer months. Pilgrims who cannot face the rigours of the traditional pilgrimage can opt for a one-day retreat instead. *(National Library of Ireland)*

The granite Round Tower on Tory Island, pictured here in 1965, is an impressive monument situated within a former ecclesiastical settlement. There are signs of change on the island. There is a television aerial on the right, a small lorry can be seen close to the Tower and telegraph poles are visible. But the old ways did not vanish overnight, and a donkey and creel can be seen on the right. *(Michael Davies)*

Ramelton Bridge, in the 1930s. Situated on the River Lennan, with a fine salmon fishery, the town has a rich architectural heritage which makes it unique in the county. Its origins lie in the Plantation period and it is closely associated with Sir William Stewart, who built forty-five houses in 1620. Much of the town's subsequent prosperity derived from its mills, bleach greens, tanyard, brewery and linen works. The beautifully preserved warehouses along the quay are a reminder of the trans-Atlantic shipping trade. *(Joseph Butler)*

The Hamiltons' family home is at Brownhall, near Ballintra, which formed part of a large estate, but in 1824 John Hamilton decided to construct a separate residence on St Ernan's Island outside Donegal town. His tenants helped build the causeway linking the house to the mainland. A stone plaque records the good relations that existed between the Hamiltons and their tenants. The house, pictured here in about 1960, is no longer in the family and is now a hotel. *(Beattie Collection)*

President Sean T. O'Kelly inspecting a guard of honour on the occasion of the official opening of the new church at Rossnowlagh Friary on 29 June 1952. In 1946 the friars took over Belalt House, formerly owned by the Trustees of the Sheil Hospital, Ballyshannon. The return of the Franciscans to the county was hailed as a great historic occasion in view of their contribution to Donegal's history over five hundred years. The friary also has a fine museum, run by the Donegal Historical Society. *(Derry Journal Newspapers)*

3

The Railways

A train steams into Ballyliffin station on what appears to be a Sunday excursion in the early 1930s. Ballyliffin, Rasheeny and Carndonagh were the most northerly stations in Ireland. Gerard Balfour, Chief Secretary for Ireland, was present for the cutting of the first sod for the extension to Carndonagh in 1899. He was a guest of Captain and Mrs McClintock of Tiernaleague House, Carndonagh. The Carndonagh Extension opened on 1 July 1901 and closed in 1935. It received some government aid and, despite taking a circuitous route, was praised as an example of good engineering. The Londonderry & Lough Swilly Railway had 99½ miles of track, from Carndonagh to Burtonport, making it the second longest narrow-gauge track in Ireland. *(Bigger/McDonald Collection)*

A Lough Swilly train steams into Carrigans station, 1965. Situated along the banks of the River Foyle, the village of Carrigans is rich in history. The eighteenth-century Dunmore House is associated with John McClintock, a captain of the Donegal Militia in 1745. *(Michael Davies)*

The 5.35 train from Derry to Strabane at St Johnston station, September 1960. The Derry–Strabane lir opened as the Londonderry & Enniskillen Railway on 19 April 1847 and closed on 15 February 1965. was built as a single line with loops at St Johnston and Carrigans but in 1904 it was made into a doub line all the way to Derry. Economic difficulties obliged it to revert to a single line again in 1932, wit only a loop connecting it to St Johnston. *(Michael Davies)*

Convoy station, Donegal, September 1957. CDR railcar no. 20 could be turned on a turntable. *(Revd John Parker)*

Passengers changing trains at Strabane station, *c.*1956. Note the two rail systems: the GNR broad gauge line and the CDR narrow gauge. The overhead passenger bridge was ignored on this occasion by the passengers, several of whom are carrying suitcases. The station was an important one for Donegal passengers. *(Revd John Parker)*

Railcar no. 20 makes another appearance, this time at Killybegs station in the 1950s. The goods shed to the right contains a large and a small wagon. The small railcar was capable of pulling up to six wagons but it was not designed for heavy loads. The trawlers to the left are a reminder of the links between the railway and the pier at Killybegs. The railways were an essential adjunct to the fishing industry here over a century ago, transporting the fish that were caught at Killybegs. *(David Lawrence)*

Stranorlar station in September 1957, shortly before the railway closed down. The freight train is pulled by the engine *Erne*. The Catholic church can be seen in the background. In 1861 a competition was held for the design of a railway station at Stranorlar. Mr Clayton of Bristol was the winner and the new station opened in September 1863. The Finn Valley Railway Company's seal was displayed over the front door of the main building. *(Norman Simmons)*

4

Offshore Islands

Arranmore Island, September 1965. The island had a population of 1,103 according to the census of 1891, but ten years later that figure was significantly higher because of a boom in the fishing industry. Arranmore is the largest inhabited island off the Donegal coast. Today there is a regular ferry service between the island and Burtonport. The cigarette advertisement on the shop to the right is bilingual, a reminder that a large number of Irish speakers used to live on the island. *(Michael Davies)*

A fisherman and a priest on board the Tory ferry in 1965. A large crowd waits on the pier, where a crane for hoisting boats from the water can be seen. Mindful of the rough seas ahead, the young priest is putting on his waterproof clothing. The island lies 11 miles from the mainland and the ferry *Tormore* takes passengers to the island daily from Bunbeg and Magheraroarty. The island boasts a 14-bedroom hotel. Visitors can see the Tau Cross and the Round Tower, and listen to stories about the Holy Clay and Balor of the Evil Eye. There is also a Wishing Stone, a bird sanctuary and a lighthouse. *(Michael Davies)*

The Tory Island curragh is a hybrid boat that incorporates various features copied from yachts visiting the island. Its gunwales were made of sections joined with galvanised boat nails. The ribs were made of oak, and canvas was used to provide a skin for the boat. The canvas was treated with tar to protect it from the sea. In this photograph, taken in 1965, two men are rowing a curragh with five passengers who had disembarked from the ferry which was unable to reach the pier due to low water. At this time getting to Tory was quite difficult because of the poor landing facilities. The photographer, Michael Davies, recalled that the boatmen carried off the boat over their heads once they had landed. *(Michael Davies)*

Magheraroarty pier, near Gortahork, is one of a number of piers used to get to Tory Island. Here the ferry is being loaded at the wooden jetty. It was unusable at low tides, and in stormy weather the island was often cut off for days. Today's modern ferry and a new pier provide a much better service. Lightkeepers who service the lighthouse on the island travel to and from the island by helicopter. *(Michael Davies)*

A crowd gathers at the pier on Tory Island in 1965 to board the ferry to the mainland, which at that time was a small fishing boat. The pier and slipway were constructed by the Congested Districts Board between 1903 and 1912 to improve communications with the island but facilities remained very basic for many years afterwards. The group includes fishermen and visitors, one of whom is carrying a suitcase. The half-decker ferry was unsuitable for large numbers but it helped to improve the islanders' case for a better ferry service and pier. *(Michael Davies)*

Tory woman uses a farm donkey to transport her household supply of fuel in September 1965. The picture is a reminder of the harshness of life on the island in the past when simple tasks such as providing fuel for cooking and heating were time-consuming and labour-intensive. Such work was often undertaken by women, especially during the fishing season when men were at sea. The roads on the island were nothing more than gravel paths at this time. *(Michael Davies)*

A Tory islander named Mr Diver bags his turf at Magheraroarty pier before taking it out to Tory, *c.* 1965. He cut the turf on the mainland. Over the centuries turf has been the main source of household fuel in Ireland. Landlords such as Benjamin Joule accused the islanders of exploiting the supply for poteen-making, but there was also a huge demand for turf a century ago when kelp was also being burned. The importance of turf declined as living conditions improved and other fuels such as gas, oil, coal and electricity came into use. There are no suitable turf banks now on the island. *(Michael Davies)*

West Town, 1965. The woman with the bucket is presumably bringing water from the village well as there was no public water supply on the island at that time. To the left is the village shop, McRuairi's which has a large collection of advertising material on display. Note the brightness of the recently whitewashed houses. Thanks to the work of the Congested Districts Board in the 1900s the standard of housing here improved dramatically. Photographs from the 1890s show a line of rough thatched dwellings. *(Michael Davies)*

A Tory farmer unloads his supply of corn, *c.* 1965. The stack is covered with netting to prevent it from being blown away, and is built close to the shed for added protection. It was difficult to grow crops of any kind on the island because of the presence of rabbits and the lack of ditches to keep out wandering livestock. A small clump of turf can be seen on the left. *(Michael Davies)*

Harvest-time on Tory, *c.* 1965. Stooks of corn can be seen on the left and the ubiquitous donkey makes another appearance. *(Michael Davies)*

This tranquil scene, *c.* 1965, illustrates the peace and beauty of the island, which attracts holidaymakers, ornithologists, geologists and painters. The renowned painter Derek Hill left his comfortable accommodation at Glebe House near Churchill to spend his summers on the island, where he found the light unique. He worked in a small hut overlooking the cliffs. As a result of his work there the Tory Island School of Painters was founded and its members have exhibited their art all over the world. Modern paintings can be seen in the island's art gallery. *(Michael Davies)*

Major McClintock walking with his dog along Inch Lake in Inishowen, August 1914. A few months later he would find himself in the trenches of the First World War. Of the 8,000 Donegal men and women who were involved, it is estimated that 1,200 lost their lives. On the battlefield he met Fr William McNeely of Donegal Town, a young Catholic chaplain who served in the British Army from 1917 to 1919 and who later became Bishop of Raphoe. They remained lifelong friends. When the major had a problem, his usual comment was 'Ask the Bishop!' *(McClintock Collection)*

5

To the Waters and the Wild

Greencastle harbour in the 1970s. The finding of worked flints locally indicates that there has been habitation here since earliest times. In the early 1800s, with the building of the fort and Martello Tower, the need for a proper pier became evident. One was duly built here in 1813 and there have been several additions to it. In the 1830s huge catches of cod and turbot and great shoals of herring brought prosperity to the area. Today the Magilligan–Greencastle car ferry brings large numbers of visitors to the fishing port. *(van der Elsen/Beattie Collection)*

The annual Moville regatta has been held in August since the middle of the nineteenth century. This picture was taken outside the Anchor Bar, close to the old Stone Pier, in about 1960. The bar was once owned by one of the main landlords in the area, the Carys. The famous novelist Joyce Cary was a member of this family; the townland of Castlecary is called after them. The one-man punt was a popular test of skill, judging by the crowds. At the halfway point contestants had to disembark, run to McKinney's Hotel, consume a bottle of porter and then return to the punt to finish the race. (*Bigger/McDonald Collection*)

Passengers on Carrickarory Pier, Moville, waiting to board the ferry *Highland Seabird* to Oban in Scotland. This service was inaugurated on 3 June 1978. The crossing took three hours and the fare was £23. Passengers were also taken on board at Portrush. Travellers enjoyed superb views of the Giant's Causeway and the islands of Islay and Jura. The official launch took place in Keaveney's Hotel and Lady Wilson, whose family owned the ferry, was present. The ferry experienced problems during severe weather and passenger numbers were lower than predicted, so few people were surprised when the service closed within a short period. The hopper on the right is a reminder of the coal boats that made deliveries here for local coal merchants during the 1960s and early 1970s. *(van der Elsen/Beattie Collection)*

Members of the Derry Port and Harbour Commissioners setting out for a short trip on Lough Foyle, in the 1930s. The boat is a drontheim, so-called because it came from Trondheim in Norway. Its unusual shape made it extremely popular with fishermen on the north coast, especially when they were entering narrow sea inlets. A drontheim can be seen today in the Inishowen Maritime Museum. *(Bigger/McDonald Collection)*

A fleet of steam drifters after landing their catch at Buncrana, *c.* 1925. The registration letters indicate that most of the boats came from Scotland: KY for Kirkcaldy and INS for Inverness. It was quite common for Scottish vessels to fish along the north coast of Donegal and land the catch at Buncrana, but in the 1920s this led to tension between Donegal and Scottish fishermen over catches and auctions of fish on the pier. *(Bigger/McDonald Collection)*

...shing vessels dock at Buncrana pier, *c.* 1945. The words 'McGrath's Restaurant and Bar' are written ... bold white lettering on the roof of the Drift Inn on the Derry Road. Built in 1864, it served at one ...me as a railway station for the town and in summer thousands arrived by train and crowded the ...aches here. A springboard, erected in 1875, was a popular attraction with amateur divers, but this ...s now been removed. The railway has also gone but visitors are still welcome in the Drift Inn for food ...d drink. The exterior remains largely unaltered and it is a fine example of a building from the great ...ilway era. *(Bigger/McDonald Collection)*

The large number of Scottish steam drifters in this magnificent photograph of Buncrana pie
c. 1927, is a reminder of the value of fishing to the Donegal economy in the early years of the last centur
The ships had tall funnels so that the steam was released well above the fishermen. They were nicknam
'woodbines' (after the cigarette) because of their shape. Each had a crew of twelve and they had a
advantage over sailing vessels because they could catch more fish. On the other hand they were expensi
to run and burned large quantities of coal. When the herring industry declined, the steam drifters becan
an expensive luxury. (*Bigger/McDonald Collection*)

The tug *Attendant* berths at Buncrana pier in the 1930s. This tug was involved in salvage work on the *Laurentic*, which struck a mine off Fanad Head in 1917 after visiting the Royal Navy's base at Lough Swilly. It was also used by the Mallet Salvage Company to try to recover the gold bars that were known to be on board the *Laurentic*. They retrieved five gold bars but, after three seasons working on the wreck, they made no further progress and the company was declared bankrupt. The *Attendant* was seized by receivers when it berthed in Derry. *(Bigger/McDonald Collection)*

Members of the Derry Port and Harbour Commissioners set sail from Port Sallagh in 1901 on Lough Foyle. *(Bigger/McDonald Collection)*

David Flynn was one of fifty sailors who lost their lives when HMS *Wasp* struck a reef off Tory Island on 23 September 1884. His job as a stoker was to maintain the fires which generated steam for the ship's engines. This photograph was taken in September 1884 just a few days before the ship was lost. *Wasp* acted as the flagship for the City of Derry Regatta and also ferried members of the Corporation down the Foyle to deliver an address to the Duke of Edinburgh on board the flagship *Minotaur*. The ship regularly visited the north-west to carry out relief duties for the Quakers during periods of distress. The photographer was Hugh Kerr, who had a studio in Carlisle Road in Derry. *(Bigger/ McDonald Collection)*

Records show that there has been a lighthouse on Arranmore since 1798, but a new lighthouse was built in 1865. Arranmore has the largest island population in the county so it has always been a popular posting for lightkeepers. The station is now automatic but the keeper arrives by helicopter to make regular maintenance checks. *(Joseph Butler)*

6

The Emigration Trail

The weekly arrival in Lough Foyle of the American liners, such as the *Caledonia*
seen here, was a source of great interest in the years before the Second World War.
Enumeration of emigrants from Irish ports began in 1851 and in the fifty-year period
ending in 1901 a total of 122,641 people emigrated from Donegal, more than half
of them men. Among the passengers to arrive in Moville was the author of *Angela's
Ashes*, Frank McCourt. His comments have not been recorded.
(Bigger/McDonald Collection)

This photograph of the Lloyd's Signal Tower on Malin Head was taken on 1 January 1902, when the buildings were bedecked with flags for the opening of the Wireless Station. The Marconi Wireless Company was commissioned by Lloyds to service six coastal stations in the British Isles. Passengers sailing from Ireland to America were able to send messages home via the new system, which replaced the old signalling system. There was also a signal station on Inistrahull Island. The modern Malin Head station nearby is still providing marine radio communications and is a major centre for the coordination of maritime rescue operations. *(National Library of Ireland)*

A family of 1930s emigrants experiences the sorrow of departure on board the *Seamore*, the local tender, before heading off to their new life overseas. Photographers in Derry were often on hand on the pier to photograph the emigrants, who came from all over Ireland and from all classes. Most Donegal exiles passed through the port of Derry. The traditional farewell party, often referred to as a 'bottling' or American Wake, went on all night. Young emigrants from West Donegal walked to Derry to catch the boat. *(Bigger/McDonald Collection)*

The tender *Seamore* ferried passengers, shown here in the 1930s, from Derry to Moville. In the deep waters of Lough Foyle, the Anchor line steamers waited for the tender before making the return trip to America. As transatlantic travellers they were entitled to reduced fares from the railway companies on their journey to Derry. Once on board the tender, there was an opportunity to listen to traditional music played by a blind fiddler from Ballyliffin. As the liners set sail, families gathered on prominent hillsides to wave goodbye. One such place was the Cairn at Greencastle, where there is now a small theatre with an audio-visual history presentation. *(Bigger/McDonald Collection)*

A large family group poses sedately for the photographer on board the *Seamore*, probably in the 1930s. From the late eighteenth century entire family groups have emigrated in search of a better life. Emigration peaked at key times such as the Great Famine and during the Land War when there were wholesale evictions. A series of poor harvests would also drive people from the land. For many, the only alternative was the workhouse. *(Bigger/McDonald Collection)*

family posing on the tender with Derry
quays in the background in the early
years of the twentieth century. This is
one of the iconic images of emigration
from the port of Derry, which took place
over many centuries. The transatlantic
trade was dominated by two Derry
families, the Cookes and the McCorkells.
The McCorkell building on the quays in
Derry was demolished some years ago.
(Bigger/McDonald Collection)

A group of passengers outside the Anchor Line Office on Foyle Street in Derry. There were agents of the shipping company in many Donegal towns, where tickets could be bought. The Anchor Tavern in Moville was originally an office for the Anchor Line. (*Bigger/McDonald Collection*)

The tender *Seamore* drawing close to an American liner anchored in Lough Foyle to await the arrival of passengers and mail destined for America, 1930s. Passengers en route to America frequently stopped off at Moville to spend a few hours sightseeing. Jarveys were on hand to provide transport and there was intense competition for business. (*Bigger/McDonaldCollection*)

7

The Sporting Life

Golfers outside Buncrana play on, undisturbed by the sound of the Lough Swilly train on the Derry–Buncrana line in the 1930s, shortly before the line closed down. The North West Golf Links was officially opened in August 1891 and boasted seventy members. Both the Lough Swilly Hotel and the Lough Swilly Railway Company helped to promote the club in the early days. A cottage in the grounds of the club was used as a clubhouse. In 1950 there were fourteen golf courses in the county but only five of them were 18-hole courses. At one of them, Rossnowlagh, Sunday play was prohibited. *(Bigger/McDonald Collection)*

Friends and family turn up to offer their support in the early days of the GAA in O'Donnell Park, Letterkenny, *c.* 1950. *(National Library of Ireland)*

An excited group of onlookers watch a game in progress at the Municipal Golf Club at Buncrana, which opened on 1 May 1926, the first to be opened by an urban council in Ireland. In 1931 Buncrana Urban Council acquired the Ballymacarry Greens for the purpose of extending the links. Three holes were made available on the extension while six were still maintained on the old links. In 1951 the club was affiliated to the Golfing Union of Ireland and in 1995 the name was changed to Buncrana Golf Club. A new clubhouse was officially opened in 2004 for the nine-hole course. *(Bigger/McDonald Collection)*

The St Johnston cricket team outside Brigade Cricket Club at Beechgrove in Waterside, Derry, in the early 1930s. The club was founded in 1898 and has the unique distinction of being the only club in the Republic of Ireland to be part of the North-West Cricket Union which covers Northern Ireland. This team appears to consist of only ten players; perhaps the umpire was counted as the eleventh. Back row, left to right: G. Lapsley (scorer), T. Orr, J. McLaughlin, J. Rankin, R. McLaughlin, J. McKean, Dan McGill. Front row: S. Alexander, J. McKean, W. Alexander, W. Quigley, B. Stevenson. *(Bigger/McDonald Collection)*

Opposite: Prizewinners displaying their silverware at the North-West Golf Club at Lisfannon, Buncrana, in the early 1930s. On the left is Sir Henry Miller, a solicitor who lived in Buncrana. He married Maud M. Meredith and had a son and four daughters. Sir Henry held the position of Town Clerk in Derry and was elected Mayor in 1901 and 1902. When his son was born he was presented with a silver cradle by Derry Corporation. He was both President and Captain of the North-West Club, and held similar positions at Portrush. He was also an enthusiastic rugby player, winning an international cap for Ireland in 1888 in the match against Scotland. He died in 1936. The Miller window can be seen in the Guildhall. *(Bigger/McDonald Collection)*

Three motocross enthusiasts pose for the camera at Bundoran, *c.* 1960. *(Jean Curran)*

Stock car racing at Bundoran, *c.* 1960. *(Jean Curran)*

8

Donegal at Work

Friesian cattle belonging to a local dairy farmer enjoying the view of the Foyle and
Magilligan in County Derry in the 1960s. Benevenagh is in the background.
(van der Elsen/Beattie Collection)

The horse and cart provided an efficient form of transport on Donegal farms for many generations and became a symbol of the small-farm economy. The state of the harness, the appearance of the horse and the traditional colours on the cart all contribute to an image of rural Ireland that has long since disappeared. By the 1950s the grey Ferguson tractor was making the horse redundant on many Donegal farms; the tarring of country roads and the increase in the volume of traffic were other factors. This photo was taken in the Letterkenny area in the 1940s. *(Jean Curran)*

The Turf Campaign. Willie McElhinney with a load of turf in south Donegal in 1942. Willie worked as a mechanic in McAuley's garage in Letterkenny and was employed as a driver for one of their lorries at this time. The Second World War had resulted in a widespread shortage of fuel and a Turf Campaign was launched by the government, administered by the County Council. New turf-cutting areas were identified and the turf was taken by lorry to the broad-gauge station at St Johnston for transportation to Phoenix Park in Dublin where it was stacked and distributed. *(Jean Curran)*

traditional horse and cart in use on a farm near Malin Head in the 1930s. Here turf sods are being
ken home for fuel. Carts were also used to transport hay and corn, take pigs to the market and milk cans
the nearest creamery. In Donegal in the 1950s most farms had two horses. The most popular breed was
e Scottish Clydesdale, which was capable of working either with a cart or with a plough. They were also
ed to pull hearses. *(Bigger/McDonald Collection)*

traditional Donegal farmyard at Glengad in Inishowen in the late 1940s. The McKenna farm was situated
1 high ground overlooking the Atlantic near Portaleen Pier. The porch was a traditional feature of rural
ouses at this time. The half-door, which is partly visible, was designed to keep out farmyard chickens and
ad the advantage of keeping the family in touch with what was happening in the farmyard outside; a
osed door was a sign that visitors were not welcome. Half-doors disappeared from rural dwellings in the
960s. *(Bigger/McDonald Collection)*

Small farmers from the Laggan area of Donegal wait in line for customs clearance for their buttermilk at the Galliagh Border Post outside Derry City, *c.* 1937. Once they had passed through Customs and Excise, they faced another obstacle: the Corporation in Derry demanded a levy of sixpence on each cart as it crossed into Northern Ireland. Farmers who sold milk under unhygienic conditions were liable to prosecution and there were regular appearances at the local courts. Note the incorrect spelling of the placename. *(Bigger/McDonald Collection)*

Sandytown, Leenankeel, in the 1940s. This picture presents an almost unreal view of rural Donegal on a summer's day after the First World War and is another gem from the Schenkel Collection. All these houses have since been re-roofed with slates. The cluster of houses was called a 'clachan'; to the casual observer they seem to have been built randomly, but in fact careful planning took account of the prevailing winds and the slope of the ground. Kitchen floors were sloped to permit water to run out of the front door when the floors were being washed. Feeding the farmyard poultry presented a problem in clachans as all the neighbours' poultry were likely to join in. Nevertheless, there was a strong community bond in each clachan and the families all came together for activities such as threshing when extra help was needed. (Bigger/McDonald Collection)

Cattle being driven along the Buncrana–Derry road at Fahan, *c.* 1936. Mitchell's shop was established in this cottage but moved to new premises in 1937. The original shop, a landmark for generations has since been demolished. The twin pillars behind the cattle mark the roadway to the home of Howard Brewster (it is now Nazareth House), who belonged to a Derry bakery family. Brewster ended his days in Roneragh House, which is now vacant; apartments overlook the old pier and the new marina. The house on the left was Baldricks. Both buildings in the picture can still be seen but the beautiful trees were removed to make way for road-widening. The cross-slab of St Mura is in the village graveyard. There used to be a railway station here which had the distinction of being the first in Ireland to have electric light. (*Bigger/McDonald Collection*)

Opposite: Farmworkers busy cutting corn with a horse-drawn mower on Mehaffey's farm near Ballindrait, *c.* 1960. An acre of corn could be cut in less than a day. Two people were required to operate the mower, with normally two others tying the sheaves. The horse-drawn Bamlett mower was popular in Donegal and was considered a great advance on the sickles and scythes of earlier generations. At the end of the day the final job was to set the sheaves in stooks of four for drying before they were built into cornstacks. Most farmhouses had several cornstacks, which were both a symbol of wealth and a source of animal feed for the winter. (*McClintock Collection*)

Fishermen at Tullagh, near Clonmany, hauling a boat to the beach after a day's fishing in 1948. This photo was taken by Ludwig Schenkel. (*Bigger/McDonald Collection*)

Members of A Company, 24th Battalion FCA, *c.* 1960. Front row, left to right: Pat McCauley, John McMonagle, John's brother Frank. Middle row: Neal Conaghan, Malachy Gormley, Jim Crawford, Eddie Crawford. Back row: Jack Foley, Pat Foley, Kevin McIntyre, Brendan McIntyre. (*McClintock Collection*

A female contestant prepares her plough for a ploughing match in Carndonagh in the 1950s. Ploughing in the traditional manner was a popular challenge in the county until the 1950s. The introduction of tractors to ploughing resulted in most old-style ploughs being abandoned in the fields, although some traditional ploughing matches are still held occasionally in the county. Less land went under the plough as farmers turned to sheep and cattle production and soon it became uneconomical for small producers to till land for potatoes. In the 1901 census 4,701 Donegal women are recorded as being employed in agriculture. *(Derry Journal Newspapers)*

A group of Donegal farmers and their supporters pose for the camera during a ploughing contest in Inishowen in the 1950s. Note that all are wearing footwear appropriate for the occasion. *(Derry Journal Newspapers)*

Ploughing match, Carndonagh, 1957. Competitor no. 2 takes a break. He is dressed in his Sunday best for the occasion. In an era when most small farmers in Donegal still had two horses, the annual ploughing match was an important social event. It was a test of skill and helped to maintain good standards of ploughmanship. Considerable numbers of farmers can be seen in the background following the progress of the competitors. In the 1901 census 48,719 persons, men and women, are recorded as working in agricultural occupations. *(Derry Journal Newspapers)*

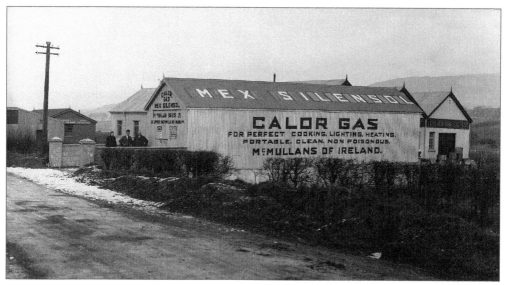

The advent of partition followed by the Economic War of the 1930s led to a number of businesses being set up at Border villages. Early arrivals in the 1930s included Mex Silensol, Calor Gas and the grocery wholesale business of O'Neill & McHenry. Part of the business premises of the latter can be seen on the right. They sold a brand of tea called Daghdha Tea, named after a pagan god. Their lorries made deliveries to dozens of small village grocery shops in north Donegal until recent times. Orders were taken by a team of 'travellers' who called on the grocers every month. *(Bigger/McDonald Collection)*

In the 1950s every farmhouse had a splash churn similar to the one seen here. Milk was conserved in crockery containers and the cream was used once a week on 'Churning Day'. Most families reserved one morning per week for churning. Country butter was sold in local shops or bartered for groceries delivered by travelling shop vans. As the job was time-consuming, it was a tradition that visitors who called to a house during churning would lend a hand with the work. This picture was taken in the 1960s, when the weekly churning custom in north Donegal was almost dead. The advent of strict hygiene regulations in food shops also contributed to the demise of the family churn. *(van der Elsen/ Beattie Collection)*

By the 1960s, when this picture was taken, the home spinning tradition was just a memory. One of the last of the traditional spinners was Cecilia Carey of Carrowbeg, in Inishowen who used wool from sheep reared on her own farm. *(Canon John McGettigan)*

Slipper John Devine taking part in the McAlevey Gold Cup, which was held at Lifford on 13 November 1962. *(Derry Journal Newspapers)*

9

Holidays in Donegal

Children enjoying a day out at Dunfanaghy, in the 1940s. *(McClintock Collection)*

Glengad Regatta. Crowds gathered at Portaleen Pier near Malin Head to watch the sailing events in 1948. Regattas were very popular along the Donegal coast when boats were more plentiful. Most of the twenty or so boats in this picture are drontheims. The annual Portaleen Regatta is now a thing of the past, partly because of the decline in the number of boats and partly as a consequence of emigration. A similar regatta was also held at Tremone. *(Bigger/McDonald Collection)*

Lough Salt in north Donegal is a tarn south of Sheephaven Bay and Mulroy, lying at 900 feet above sea-level. Its Irish name is Cnoc a Liathain. Traditionally it was one of the famous assembly points for young people on 'Blueberry Sunday', the name applied to both the Sunday before and the Sunday after the first day of August. People came from the parishes of Termon, Kilmacrennan, Meevagh and Doe to dance to the music of local fiddlers. Such assemblies died out with the coming of the First World War. This photograph shows a group visiting Lough Salt in 1950. With the increased popularity of the motor car, it became a popular venue for picnics and family outings. The lake is a major source of water for Letterkenny. *(McClintock Collection)*

Edith McClintock and some family friends enjoying a summer picnic near Dunfanaghy, *c.* 1935. *(McClintock Collection)*

This unusual photograph, taken on the Dunfanaghy course, illustrates the early history of golf in Donegal. The style of dress of the players and guests indicates that the photograph was taken between 1890 and 1895. *(David Bigger)*

Opposite above: Children from Letterkenny enjoying a day in the bog helping to draw turf. Donkey were particularly useful for drawing turf from wet boglands before tractors were introduced for th purpose. *(McClintock Collection)*

Opposite below: Members of the McClintock family and some friends enjoying a summer picnic in th 1950s. Horn Head and Dunfanaghy Pier are in the background. *(McClintock Collection)*

A motorbike enthusiast setting off on a journey in Donegal in the 1960s. (*Jean Curran*)

Moville Regatta, 1880s. This rare photograph of a very competitive boat race shows four teams heading towards the Stone Pier. Huge crowds are standing on the banks. The Prospect Hotel can be seen on the right; now a bar, it retains the name. Montgomery Terrace, completed in 1884, consists of only two houses here so the photograph must date from the early 1880s. It is definitely before 1887 as St Eugene's Temperance Hall has not been constructed. *(Bigger/McDonald Collection)*

A firing party prepares to salute a bride and groom. The location is not known but the photograph was taken in the 1930s. The tradition of firing a single round as a token of good luck before a wedding still survives in some rural townlands in Donegal. On this occasion the firing party is a very large one. The last time the author witnessed such an event was in the 1970s. *(Bigger/McDonald Collection)*

Well-dressed bikers take a trip along the coast in June 1950. *(Jean Curran)*

A scenic view along the Corkscrew Road overlooking Mulroy Bay, *c.* 1940. Scenes such as these draw thousands of visitors to the county annually. It was on the shores of this bay that the 3rd Earl of Leitrim was assassinated in 1878 as he travelled from his home at Manor Vaughan to Letterkenny. One of the largest landowners in Donegal, he was an unpopular landlord. *(Joseph Butler)*

10

Glencolmcille

Glencolmcille, 1900. The Congested Districts Board reported in 1892 that labourers here earned £11 per year; weaving, spinning and lobster fishing provided employment for others. The Board aimed to increase farm output and to improve the quality of tweed. A young priest, Fr McDyer, was appointed here in 1951 and very soon discovered that these objectives had not been achieved. He identified five principal problems that faced the parish in the early 1950s, which he called the 'five curses': a lack of a public water supply, untarred roads, no dispensary, no electricity and no industry. He was a determined man, however, and successfully dealt with each of the issues raised. Today the area is one of the most popular in Donegal with visitors. *(National Library of Ireland)*

Éamon de Valera takes a stroll in the show field at Glencolmcille in September 1955. With him are Fr McDyer CC (Chairman) and Cormac Breslin, Leas-Ceann Comhairle of the Dáil. The show attracted 700 entries, with categories for cattle and ponies, poultry and eggs, vegetables and farm products, honey and fruit. There were also classes for cake-making, jams, embroidery, butter and rug-making. Gaeltarra Eireann had a special exhibition in the Halla Mhuire. Among the judges were Captain Tindal of Ballyloughan House, Bruckless, Victor Crawford of Pettigo and Miss Ita McGeehan of Letterkenny. *(Derry Journal Newspapers)*

The guard of honour welcomed Éamon de Valera and his companions to the annual show on 2 September 1955. They were on their way to view the County Donegal Committee of Agriculture exhibit at Cashel School. Schoolchildren waved tricolours and there were banners in the streets to welcome de Valera. *(Derry Journal Newspapers)*

A guard of honour made up of surviving members of the Old IRA takes up position before being inspected by Éamon de Valera at the Annual Show at Glencolmcille in September 1955. Fr McDyer spoke about the number of projects that had come to fruition as a result of representations he had made to Mr de Valera and Major Costello of Gaeltarra Eireann. *(Derry Journal Newspapers)*

Éamon de Valera addressing the crowd at the opening of the annual show at Glencolmcille in September 1955. From left to right: Fr J. McDyer CC (Chairman), Mrs J.J. McGinley (Treasurer), Mr P. McGinley (Secretary) and Dáil deputies Cormac Breslin and Joseph Brennan. De Valera encouraged the use of the Irish language, remarking: 'If there is one area where the Gaelic language can be saved, it is here, where the people are willing to help themselves. Every effort must be made to save the language in the Gaeltacht and provide employment.' He also praised Muintir na Tíre. Much of this work is continued today by the Folk Museum and Oideas Gael. *(Derry Journal Newspapers)*

Glencolmcille cabins, 1900. In this picture taken by Robert Welsh there are contrasting images of housing conditions in Glencolmcille. In the foreground there is a thatched one-roomed stone-built cabin and in the background a well maintained two-roomed thatched cottage with white-washed walls and a large, securely roofed outbuilding. In 1892, an Inspector of the Congested Districts Board named Townsend Gahon described housing conditions as 'very inferior'; in his opinion, the outside was better than the inside. Fires were kept burning in winter and summer.

A number of stray sheep can be seen on the roadway. They were probably Scottish Blackface sheep which produced wool of poor quality. Although no poultry can be seen, eggs were important in a cashless society and were bartered in local shops for tea, sugar, tobacco and oatmeal. The clothing worn by the four women seen here would have been homemade; cloth for Sunday wear could be bought from travelling salesmen called 'pack-men'. Corduroy trousers were popular for men and on Sundays women wore shawls.

Roads like the one in the picture were generally good and were maintained by local relief schemes. Although the district is near the sea, it was difficult to develop fisheries because of the high cliffs and the lack of a harbour. The large cart seen in the centre was probably used by several families. The land behind the cabins was used as a commonage where each householder could graze a few sheep or a cow. The area a family could graze was known as a 'cow's grass'. (Ulster Museum)

11

All Sides of Life

The Rosguill Band, *c.* 1952. *(Derry Journal Newspapers)*

The Convoy Pipe Band, 1944, pictured on the steps of the Guildhall in Derry after taking part in a competition there. The Drum Major is Alfred Watson of Convoy. The band originated over a century ago. In 1933 it was attired in new uniforms with green jackets and Black Watch tartan. In 1968 the village of Convoy hosted a national Pipe Band and Drum Major Competition, and in recent years the village band has visited many towns in Ireland and abroad. (*Bigger/McDonald Collection*)

Carrigans Pipe Band in the 1940s. Pipe bands such as these took part in the traditional July parades in Donegal and Derry. In some villages, where the musicians came from different religious backgrounds, they often loaned their instruments to other bands if they needed them. (*Bigger/McDonald Collection*)

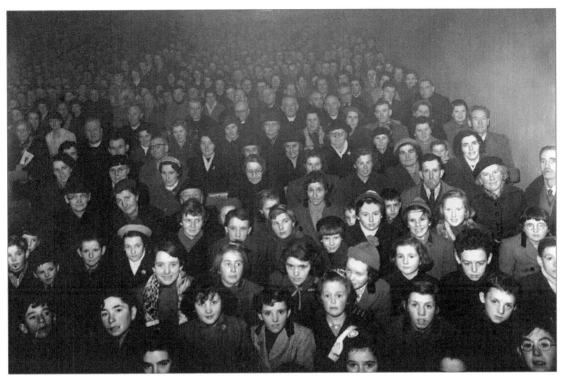

The opening of the new Parochial Hall at Crossroads in Killygordon, December 1955. *(Derry Journal Newspapers)*

r Neil Farren, Bishop of Derry, speaking at the opening of the new hall. *(Derry Journal Newspapers)*

Anna Birney taking the title role in *Dick Whittington*, with Enda Conaghan playing the role of his Cat, at the Devlin Hall, 11 January 1956. *(Derry Journal Newspapers)*

Anna Ronaghan as the 'Fairy Queen' in a scene from *Dick Whittington* on 16 January 1956. Letterkenn now has a new theatre, An Grianán, which provides a wide range of entertainment. *(Derry Journa Newspapers)*

Killygordon and Ballybofey children taking part in *Sleeping Beauty* at Killygordon, 1955. *(Derry Journal Newspapers)*

The scene outside the County Headquarters at Lifford on the occasion of the arrival of a new mobile mass X-ray unit in the mid-1950s. The scourge of tuberculosis brought devastation to many families in the county in the fifties but with the introduction of new drugs and mass radiography the disease was brought under control. In 2000 just nine cases were reported in the North-West Health Board, which includes Donegal, and the county has one of the lowest rates in Ireland. T.F. O'Higgins, Minister for Health, is pictured with County Secretary T. McManus, Dr Eustace, Dr Coyne, Denis Flanagan, Hugh McKendrick, John Coll and several county councillors. *(Derry Journal Newspapers)*

Students outside Crossconnell National School at Clonmany in the 1880s. The girls are attired in pinafores while many of the boys wear waistcoats or petticoats. In good weather, children often went to school barefoot. The teacher is Barney Doherty. *(McGlinchey School Clonmany)*

Greencastle Harbour in the 1950s, before development work was undertaken. The Coastguard Station which incorporates the Inishowen Maritime Museum, can be seen in the background. The museum chronicles the maritime life of the region and offers some fine exhibits, photographs, maps and charts. In addition there is a planetarium. *(Derry Journal Newspapers)*

In February 1922 a new police force took over control of policing in the Irish Free State from the Royal Irish Constabulary. Here, Garda Hugh Beatty is seen in May 1922, following his appointment at the age of 26. He was on duty for the funerals of Michael Collins and Arthur Griffith in Dublin, and he was also on duty when the new Dáil Eireann was in session. Large numbers joined the Civic Guards from Donegal, including ten young men from Carrowmena district. Beatty was among the earliest recruits and his registration number was 1455. He had worked on the family farm before his recruitment. When he retired in 1953 he had served for thirty-one years and one day. *(Beattie Collection)*

A group of school children on the steps of Culdaff House, May 1888, from Miss Campbell's school, Culdaff. Hedge schools were still common in the district in the early years of the nineteenth century. A student of one of them, Charles Macklin (*c.* 1697–1797), went on to become a famous actor and playwright in London. An Autumn School has been held in his honour in Culdaff every October since 1990. *(Bigger/ McDonald Collection)*

The Revd Kane (standing centre), Dunfanaghy, *c.* 1880. A native of County Derry, he had considerable success in fund-raising activities for the church building fund. Because of his initiative and energy, he was often referred to as a 'one-man band'. *(Bigger/McDonald*

Members of the Berry and Schenkel families enjoying a meal in Gallen's Inishowen Hotel, Clonmany, in September 1958. A full lunch was served for 7 shillings and 6 pence. This photograph is from the Ludwig Schenkel Collection and was taken by William Pointz. Tom Berry (standing, right) was a teacher in Culmore; Ludwig (seated, left) was an Austrian Jew who fled to Ireland during the Anschluss and set up a manufacturing business called Halliday's in Foyle Street, Derry, which exported rexine bags to Nigeria. Harrods of London were also customers. He loved the piano, photography and nature, and spent his holidays in Urris. Seated, left to right: Ludwig Schenkel, Marion Berry, Inez Pointz, Ita Gallen, Loni Schenkel. Standing: Pat Gallen, Tom Berry. *(Bigger/McDonald Collection)*

Carndonagh station, 1992. This beautiful building has recently been restored, having served as a dwelling-house and offices for a number of years. The first train arrived here in 1901. The railway faced difficulties associated with the First World War and the Civil War so it was not a surprise when it closed in 1935. A number of former railway cottages and bridges remain. The chimney belongs to the Alcohol Factory which has since been demolished. *(Beattie Collection)*

Staff and students outside Glencrow National School, Moville, in 1888. This building is now a private residence. *(Bigger/McDonald Collection)*

Members of Burt Presbyterian Bible Class, 1875. In 1870 there were 1,094 Presbyterian Sunday Schools registered. The population of the county in 1881 was 206,035; 76 per cent were Catholic, 12 per cent were Church of Ireland and 10 per cent were Presbyterian. Early settlers founded a congregation here in 1673, forming part of the Laggan Presbyterian community. Sir Robert Ferguson, whose statue once stood in the Diamond in Derry, was a great-grandson of a Burt minister, while Derry's Brooke Park is named after another Burt minister. *(Bigger Collection)*

Members of Clonmany Local Defence Force, 1941. During the war the LDF acted as auxiliaries to the army. In the centre is Patrick Kavanagh, a local schoolmaster who collected folklore from a weaver called Charles McGlinchey and published it in *The Last of the Name*. The McGlinchey Summer School is held in Clonmany to celebrate the history and culture of the area. *(McGlinchey Summer School)*

The Donegal Grand Jury in March 1899, just months before it ceased to function, its role being taken over by the County Council. Its members were Major James Hamilton (Foreman), Ernest Cochrane, Sir James Musgrave, Robert McClintock, Charles Stewart, Francis Macky, William Hamilton, J.C. McClintock, Captain William Knox, John Hamilton, Robert Moore, Arthur Wallace, Henry Stubbs, Thomas Colquhoun, Robert Crawford, Captain Thomas Stoney, T. Humphreys, J. McFarlane, Captain John Riky, Major John Baillie, John Pomeroy and J. Grove (Secretary). *(Donegal County Council Archives)*

This studio photograph from the 1880s is entitled 'Miss Montgomery's Group' from Moville. It has not been possible to name them individually. An insight into social life in Moville is found in the diary of Jane Harvey, who spent August 1876 in Drumaweir near Greencastle. One of the big events of the summer season was the Moville Flower Show, which was promoted mainly by the gentry. The Regatta took place on 8 August and enjoyed a wider appeal. After listening to the band of the 91st Regiment of Highlanders, in the evening Jane went to a ball at Kilderry, Muff, which ended at 5.20 am. She knew Ferguson Montgomery, a keen sportsman who organised games of tennis and croquet for the ladies on the front lawns of New Park, watched by his parents, Sir Robert and Lady Montgomery. Jane's son James preferred cricket, however, and he played a weekly match at Pennyburn. Bathing took place at Drumaweir and afterwards everyone boarded the Harts' boat for Moville. In the evenings Lady Montgomery was busy organising concerts and games of whist in the schoolhouse or parlour for her guests. On Sundays Jane attended both morning and evening church services and listened to the sermon of the young Henry Montgomery, later Bishop of Tasmania. She described him as impressive but felt he did a better job in the morning. When her holiday ended, she took the evening steamer from Moville back to Derry. *(Bigger Collection)*

The weaving industry was revived in Clonmany parish in the 1950s by a group of local businessmen and a priest, Fr Mullan. In this photograph, taken in Harkin's former egg store in 1958, a group admires the new machinery for the tweed factory. Note the electric light and standard shade installed by the ESB in the mid-1950s. The instructor was Seamus Cannon of Glencolmcille and the guest of honour was Miss O'Neill. Also present were Willie Gordon, Jim McGonigle, John McLaughlin, Paddy McGonigle, Colm Doherty, Jimmy Ivers, Michael Doherty, Paddy Doherty, Hugh Gallagher, Thomas McGonigle, Barney O'Donnell and George Devlin. *(McGlinchey Summer School)*

The Clonmany postmen and gardai outside the post office in 1923. The car is a Model T Ford owned by publican John Campbell. Reminders of British rule can still be seen, such as the postmen's uniform, the sign and the postbox. The postmen were Paddy Grant and Mr Toland and the young girls were John Campbell's daughters. The Postmistress was Annie Friel. *(McGlinchey Summer School)*

On 10 October 1923 Robert Anderson, a Ballyshannon merchant, married Ethel Armitage of Tipperary, who worked in Bundoran. William Bigger was the best man and L. Ebbitt was the bridesmaid. Also in the picture are Willie Patterson, Francis Graham, Thompson Anderson and Ballyshannon shopkeepers Harry Lipsett and Richard Vaughan. Louis Griffith is the young boy. He later married Pattie Corscadden, a first cousin of Hazel Corscadden, mother of the British Prime Minister Tony Blair. Canon Tarleton conducted the ceremony. The Andersons went on to have four children, Betty, Alfie, Peggy (Ballyshannon) and Robert (Canada). *(Bigger Collection)*

The Anderson wedding party arriving at the Imperial Hotel in Ballyshannon for the reception. The hotel proprietors were the Miss Evans, who sold it in 1938 to the Dorrian family, the present owners. Built in 1781, it attracted a largely military clientele as Ballyshannon was a garrison town. It was also popular with the Duchess of Aberdeen. The Black Lion has connections with the 28th Regiment. Three uniformed personnel can be seen in the group viewing the guests. Wedding parties were often photographed on the steps outside the hotel, but these have now been partly removed. The hotel opposite was the Royal Millstone, which is now vacant. *(Bigger Collection)*

Bishop Farren visiting the troops at Leenan Fort in March 1940. On his right is Major-General Sweeney and on his left is Colonel McKinney, Director of Medical Services. Other clergymen present are Fr Devine, Fr McKenna (Culdaff), Fr Reid, Fr Gallagher and Fr McCauley. The Bishop also visited Dunree Fort where he blessed the shamrock and inspected a Guard of Honour. In 1940 there were 146 troops stationed at Leenan during the Emergency Period. The fort closed in 1946 and is now a ruin. Its neighbour, Dunree Fort, is now a military museum. *(Derry Journal Newspapers/McGlinchey Summer School)*

e Derry Garrison Drag Hunt was a familiar sight during the winter season in the Laggan and Border
eas of Donegal. Meets regularly took place at Burt in the 1930s but the advent of war brought such
ents to an end. Here, a party sets off in full regalia. The van in the picture belonged to Pattersons of
tterkenny, who were butchers. *(Bigger/McDonald Collection)*

e Derry Garrison Drag Hunt also held regular meets at Newtowncunningham in the 1930s and they
e seen here outside Peter McLaughlin's bar. Soldiers brought their horses from Derry overnight and
ey were stabled nearby. Hunting was confined to officers, who wore red jackets and black caps. The
mile route was marked out earlier in the day by dragsmen, who pulled along a bag of rags soaked in
iseed oil. The thatched house belonged to the Ferrys. *(Bigger/McDonald Collection)*

Set up in 1854, the Derry Port and Harbour Commission comprised fifteen elected members, the May of Derry and a Corporation member. They were responsible for all shipping on the Foyle and the pil who guided the ships. In summer one meeting was held in Greencastle, the commissioners travelli down from Derry by boat. The picture shows members and friends assembled at the Fort Hotel, owned Miss Eileen Bennet, in about 1965. They landed at the Stone Pier and a social evening usually follow Prominent Derry businessmen were invited as guests. The Revd Telford, Rector of Moville, and Lia McCormick, are also seen here. *(Bigger Collection)*

Kathleen E.M. Houston returns from a social call to her home in the Moyle, Manorcunninghan *c.* 1920. She married J.K. Bovaird of Dernaclally, Carrigans. She died in 1980. *(Bigger Collection)*

The Revd William Boyd, pictured on the occasion of his installation with Burt choir. Ordained in 1932, he served in Burt before moving to Armagh in 1939. Front row, left to right: Kitty Gamble, Mrs Miller, Bessie Love, Emily Poole. Middle row: Alice McNutt, Maggie Buchanan, Greta Boyd, Crissie Gamble, V. Bryce, Sarah Brown. (*Bigger/McDonald Collection*)

Harry Swan (left), the Donegal author, miller and antiquarian. He lived at Ardeelan, Buncrana, and his first publication was the *Book of Inishowen* which was printed by William Doherty of Buncrana in 1938. Second from right is the Revd Farquhar Orr, Minister at Buncrana Presbyterian Church (1931–52) and also a part-time lecturer in Classics at Magee College, Derry. His son Norman, the church organist, stands next to Harry Swan; he worked as a draughtsman with Derry Corporation. (*Bigger/McDonald Collection*)

This fancy dress parade was held in the Bay Field at Moville following a football match in the 1940s. Taking part were Jackie McMonagle, P.J. Doran, Joe Martin, Alfie Chapman (taking the salute), 'Quebec' (unidentified), George Walls, John Whitters (the sailor) and a 'Top Hat Man' (unidentified). *(Bigger/McDonald Collection)*

One of the main attractions of the Sunday afternoon football matches in the Bay Field in Moville was the presence of international Scottish players. Large crowds regularly travelled over from Scotland for the games. A parade was held through the town before the match, with floats and a fancy dress competition. In this 1940s photograph two wet-nurses take two 'babies' to the match in a four-wheeled iron pram owned by a local resident. The destination is obvious. Notice the horseman following behind. *(Bigger/McDonald Collection)*

Members of the Carndonagh Royal Irish Constabulary pose for the camera in the studio of Hugh Kerr in Derry in the 1880s. They are wearing helmets and carrying haversacks. It is thought they were in Derry on duty and took advantage of the occasion to have their photograph taken. In his records Kerr described them as 'Constable Irvine's group'. He did a steady business in portraits of clients from Donegal, especially those from the wealthy farming and business community. *(Bigger Collection)*

Situated on the banks of the Foyle the village of Carrigans is rich in history. The eighteenth-century Dunmore House is associated with John McClintock, a captain in the Donegal Militia in 1745. The village school at the end of the street closed in the 1940s. Harkin's and Wilkins' spirit/grocery shop can be seen on the right. Wilkins' coal shed is on the left and the two coal delivery carts probably belong to Wilkins. *(Bigger/McDonald Collection)*

Edward J. Miliffe and Catherine O'Donnell on their wedding day, 16 October 1940, at St Conal's Church, Glenties. The groom worked in a bank and the bride was from the Highlands Hotel in the town. The priest is Father Columba Haurahan, an Oblate from Athlone. The groom was also the Assistant District Leader of the Local Security Force, which later became the LDF. His colleagues provided a guard of honour and a musical salute. Ernest Foy of Athlone and Mary Boyce of Borris-in-Ossory were the witnesses. *(National Library of Ireland)*

In the 1860s Dr Walter Bernard, a Derry doctor who resided in Buncrana, became increasingly concerned about the dilapidated state of the stone fort at Grianán. In the 1870s a Derry group called the Irish Irelanders paraded from Derry to the site on Sunday afternoons and carried out repairs. The Gaelic League and GAA also lent a hand. Eventually Dr Bernard took charge of the reconstruction in person and in 1878 the work was completed at his own expense. He was confident that it would, in his own words, 'last for ages'. A tourist road to the fort was opened on Sunday 18 September 1955 by Pat O'Donnell TD and Éamon de Valera. An open-air céilidhe was held after the ceremony. *(Bigger/McDonald Collection)*

The Binns of Carndonagh were prominent shirt manufacturers in the town. This image is from the Kerr studio in Derry and shows Mrs Binns with her two daughters in 1882. Note the different styles of dress between mother and daughters. Their house was called Hopefield and the buildings at the back of it were used for the collection and distribution of cloth for shirt-making. It was later used as a Parochial House but was demolished to make way for an extension to Carndonagh Community School. *(Bigger/ McDonald Collection)*

ACKNOWLEDGEMENTS

I wish to express my sincere thanks to the following people for their help in the compilation of this book and for allowing me access to their collections of photographs: Marie Barret, Eva, Conor and John Beattie, Antony Begley, David Bigger, Nan and Patricia Brennan, Niamh Brennan, Seamus Browne, Joseph Butler, Robert Carey, George Clarke, Pat Conaghan, Sean Crawford, Canon Crooks, Jean Curran, Michael Davies, Larry Doherty, Lorcan Doherty, Thomas Doherty, Benny Dorrian, Pat Dunleavy, Peggy Eager, Kathleen Emerson, A. van der Elsen, John Farren, Patricia Faulkner, Jim Gallagher, Liam Harkin, Marius Harkin, Michael Herron, David Hume, Colán McArthur, Dessie McCallion, Charlie McCann, May McClintock, Vincent McGowan, Hazel McIntyre, Alison McLaughlin, Dermot McLaughlin, Jim McLaughlin, Peter McLaughlin, Joseph McNulty, Fr Pádraig Ó'Baoill, Anne O'Dowd, Billy Patterson, Charmaine Patton, Joseph Peoples, Fr Prendergast, Leonard Roarty, Liam Ronayne, Fr Silke, Dick Sinclair and Gerard Ward. I am especially grateful to David Bigger for his invaluable advice and cooperation and for giving me access to the Bigger/McDonald Collection and his own personal archive. Without his assistance, this publication would not have been possible.

I am grateful to the following insititutions for their cooperation and advice: the National Museum of Ireland – Country Life, Donegal County Council Archives, the National Library of Ireland, Ulster Museum, WELB Library staff at the Foyle Street Branch, Donegal County Library staff in Letterkenny, Buncrana and Carndonagh, National Military Archives, Port and Harbour Commissioners in Derry, Derry Journal Newspapers, McGlinchey Summer School, Donegal Historical Society, Raphoe Diocesan Archives, Rockhill Army Barracks and Inishowen Maritime Museum.

I acknowledge the following authors and publishers whose work I consulted: Brian Bonner, Conal Byrne, Bishop Edward Daly, David Dickson, Charlie Doherty, Louis Emerson, Estyn Evans and Brian Turner, Sheila Friel, Leslie Lucas, Canon Maguire Maghtochair, W.A. Maguire, Donald Martin, Fr McDyer, Joe McGarrigle, Lochlann McGill, Nial McGinley, Neil McGrory, John McLaughlin, the editors and authors of *Donegal History and Society* and the *Donegal Annual*, Stuart Norris, Finbar O'Connor, J. Scoltock and R. Cossum, Harry Swan.

I wish to thank the staff at Sutton Publishing for their help, especially Sarah Bryce, Michelle Tilling, Matthew Brown and Reuben Davison.